I0006180

Simply
HTML5
How To Visual Guide

By eBookLingo.com

Easy To Learn Visually Illustrated Step-By-Step Tutorials

Simply HTML5 - How To Visual Guide
By eBookLingo.com

Copyright © 2020 eBookLingo, All Rights Reserved.

Books Examples
All the examples found in this book can be found at this books supporting website at **https://www.ebooklingo.com**. Examples in this book may appear different in your browser since CSS style sheets were used when displaying the examples.

Corrections
If you find any typos or tutorials that need corrections or improvements that you feel will be beneficial to this or the website, you can contact us at the following email address at **corrections@ebooklingo.com**.

Notice of Rights
All rights reserved. No part of this book may be reproduced or transmitted in any way or form by any means including electronic, mechanical, digital, photocopying, recording, taping, informational storage, retrieval system, or otherwise, without the prior written permission of the publisher except in the case of small quotations included in critical articles or reviews.

Notice of Liability
The author and publisher have made every effort and precaution in the creation of this book to ensure the accuracy of the books information. However, the author and publisher as well as the dealers or distributors will not be held liable for any errors or omissions or for changes that may be caused either directly or indirectly resulting from the use of the information contained in this book herein, or by the software or hardware products described herein.

Notice of Trademarks
All the trademarks found herein are acknowledged as belonging to their respective owner with no intention of infringement of the trademark. This book or eBookLingo the names only in an editorial fashion for the benefit of the trademark owner.

///l ebook/ingo

Published by eBookLingo
Web: www.ebooklingo.com

Table Of Contents

Chapter 4 - HTML Forms 46

Chapter 7 - HTML Audio & Video 84

Chapter 8 - HTML Links 89

Chapter 9 - HTML Lists 112

Chapter 10 - HTML Tables 120

Chapter 11 - HTML Semantics 140

HTML Getting Started

HTML is the main markup language for describing the structure of web pages designed to be displayed in a web browser.

Here is a list of some of the things you can do with HTML.

- You can publish documents online with text, images, lists, tables, etc.

- You can access content on the web such as images, videos, or other HTML documents via hyperlinks.

- You can create web forms to collect user data like the user's name, email address, phone number, review, comments, etc.

- You can include images, videos, sound clips, flash movies, applications, and other HTML documents directly inside an HTML document.

- You can create offline content such as an offline version of your website that works even without the internet.

An HTML file is just simply a text file saved with an .html or .htm extension.

Creating The HTML File

First, you will need to open your computer's plain text editor such as Notepad (on Windows), TextEdit (on Mac), or some other type of simple text editor. Once you understand the basics of HTML, you can then use a more advanced web development tool such as Adobe Dreamweaver.

Now open up your computer's plain text editor of your choice and create a new empty file. And type the following code in the empty files window:

```
<!DOCTYPE html>
<html lang="en">
<head>
  <title>Simply HTML5</title>
</head>
<body>
  <p>Hello World!</p>
</body>
</html>
```

Example 1

Example as seen in FireFox 80.0.1 (64-bit) browser.

Hello World!

Now save the file to your desktop as `any-name.html` or any name you wish to name your HTML file. When using Notepad to save your HTML file it will normally save your files as `.txt`. But since you're writing in HTML, you will need to save the file as `.html` or `.htm`. If you do not do this, your file will be saved as a text file that will have some HTML code in it.

1. Click on File in Notepad and then Save As.
2. Find the folder you want to save to.
3. Now change the Save as type: drop-down menu to All Files (*.*)
4. Next name your file. Make sure to include the `.html` or `.htm` extension e.g. `examplepage.html`.

Now to view your HTML file in a browser. Find the file you just saved and then double click on it. It will then open in your default Web browser. If your HTML file does not open at all, open your browser and drag and drop the HTML file into it.

Code Explained

- The `<!DOCTYPE html>` is the document type declaration that tells the Web browser that the file is an HTML5 file. The declaration is case-insensitive.

- The `<html lang="en">` element is the root element of an HTML page. The attribute `lang="en"` specifies the language of the file, which in this case is English `"en"`. You can declare other languages like `"es"` for Spanish, `"fr"` for French, and so on.

- The `<head>` element contains the tags that provide meta information about the HTML file. For example, the `<title>` tag defines the title for the HTML file.

- The `<title>` element specifies a title for the HTML file.

- The `<body>` element is where all the magic happens it contains the HTML files visible content that will be displayed in the browser.

- The `<p>` element defines a paragraph.

HTML Tags

HTML tags are the starting and ending parts of an HTML element. They begin with the left angle bracket `<` and end with right angle bracket `>` . Every HTML tag is made up of a keyword surrounded by angle brackets, for example, `<title>` , `<p>` and so on. HTML tags usually come in pairs, for example, `<title>` `</title>` , `<p>` `</p>` and so on. With some exceptions like the `<img>` and `<meta>` tags and so on. These tags are referred to as empty elements, self-closing elements or void elements.

The first tag in a pair is often called the opening tag (or start tag), for example, `<p>` and the second tag is called the closing tag (or end tag) with a slash `/` after the opening left angle bracket of the closing tag, for example, `</p>` this is done in order to tell the browser that the command has been completed.

So, basically HTML tags are just an opening tag (or start tag) and a closing tag (or end tag) as seen in the example below.

```
<p><p>
```

Example 2

HTML Elements

Now an HTML element consists of both the opening and closing tags as well as the content that is between the opening and closing tags. But like I said before there are some exceptions like the `<img>` and `<meta>` tags and so on. These tags are referred to as empty elements, self-closing elements, or void elements.

Here is an example of the HTML `<p>` element below.

```
<p>This is an element.</p>
```

Example 3

Example as seen in FireFox 80.0.1 (64-bit) browser.

This is an element.

Now here is an example of an empty HTML `<hr>` element below.

```
<hr>
```

Example 4

Example as seen in FireFox 80.0.1 (64-bit) browser.

In the above example, the empty HTML `<hr>` element which stands for horizontal rule and is used to insert a horizontal rule or a thematic break in an HTML page to divide or separate sections of the web page.

An empty HTML element does not need to include a slash `/` to be valid but if you do include a slash it must come after the keyword and before the right angle bracket `>`. The following empty HTML `<hr>` elements below can be coded in the following ways and still be valid.

```
<hr/>
<hr />
<hr>
```

Example 5

Example as seen in FireFox 80.0.1 (64-bit) browser.

HTML Attributes

HTML elements can also have attributes which provide additional information about the HTML element or adjust the behavior of the HTML element. HTML attributes must be placed within the element's opening tag.

Here is a little bit of information below that you should know about HTML attributes.

- All HTML elements can have attributes.

- HTML attributes provide additional information about the HTML element.

- HTML attributes always need to be placed in the opening tag.

- HTML attributes typically come in name/value pairs, for example, `name="value"`.

- You can place multiple HTML attributes within the opening tag each attribute must have space between each other, for example, `name="value" name="value"`

- HTML attributes can also have both single and double quotes for quoting values, for example, `name="value"` and `name='value'` are both valid.

- HTML attributes values are generally case-insensitive, except for the `id` and `class` attributes values. It's generally good practice for the attributes values to be in lowercase.

Now here is how to place an HTML attribute inside the `<p>` element's opening tag below.

```
<p dir="rtl">This is an element with an HTML attribute.</p>
```

Example 6

Example as seen in FireFox 80.0.1 (64-bit) browser.

.This is an element with an HTML attribute

In the above example, the `<p>` element has the `dir` attribute placed in it which is an enumerated attribute that sets the direction of the text within the element in the HTML file. The `dir` attribute in the example above has its value set to `rtl` which means the direction of the text will be set from right to left and is to be used for languages that are written from the right to the left like Arabic for instance.

Now here is how to place multiple HTML attributes inside the `<p>` element's opening tag below.

```
<p dir="rtl" title="Element With Multiple Attributes">This is an element with multiple HTML attributes.</p>
```

Example 7

The `title` attribute in the example above will just simply specify extra information about the HTML element and when placing the mouse pointer over the element with the `title` attribute in it will display a tooltip to the user in most browsers. Remember to add a space between each attribute.

Uppercase Or Lowercase HTML Tags And Attributes

In HTML the tag and attribute names are not case-sensitive but most attribute values are case-sensitive, for example, the `id` and `class` attributes values are case-sensitive. So, in other words, this means that an HTML tag like the `<p>` tag can be coded in uppercase `<P>` or lowercase `<p>` and both styles will still define the same thing in HTML which is a paragraph.

```
<p>Valid lowercase tags.</p>
<P>Valid uppercase tags.</P>
```

Example 8

Example as seen in FireFox 80.0.1 (64-bit) browser.

Valid lowercase tags.

Valid uppercase tags.

After saying all that it's considered good practice to use lowercase for all your HTML tags and attributes.

Nesting HTML Elements

HTML elements can also be nested which means elements can contain other elements. Placing one element inside another is called nesting. Nested elements are also called child elements and can also be a parent element too if other elements are nested within it.

The following example demonstrates two examples of nested elements.

```
<p>This paragraph contains some <strong>strong</strong> text.</p>
<p>This paragraph contains some <b><i>bold and italic</i></b> text.</p>
```

Example 9

Example as seen in FireFox 80.0.1 (64-bit) browser.

This paragraph contains some **strong** text.

This paragraph contains some ***bold and italic*** text.

It's important to remember that HTML tags should be nested in the correct order. Which basically means that the last tag opened must be closed first.

I will show you the correct and wrong way to nest HTML elements in the following example.

```
<p>This is the <strong>correct</strong> way to nest elements.</p>
<p>This is the <strong>wrong</p> way to nest elements.</strong>

<p>This is the <b><i>correct</i></b> way to nest elements.</p>
<p>This is the <b><i>wrong</b></i> way to nest elements.</p>
```

Example 10

Adding Comments In HTML

HTML comments are usually added in order to make the source code easier to understand, for example, when you want to edit or have another developer edit your source code in the future. HTML comments are not displayed in the browser.

An HTML comment begins with the left angle bracket `<` followed by an exclamation point `!` and then two minus signs followed by a space `--` which creates the opening tag (or start tag), for example, `<!--` , we then close the comment by adding a space followed by two minus signs `--` and then followed by the right angle bracket `>` which creates the closing tag (or end tag), for example, `-->` . You can then place almost anything between the closing and ending comment tags except for other comments.

You can add single line HTML comments or you can add multi-line HTML comments to your HTML file as seen in the following example.

```
<!-- This is a single line comment -->
<!-- This is a
 multi-line HTML comment
 that spans across three lines -->
<p>This paragraph will be displayed in the browser.</p>
```

Example 11

You can also comment out part of your HTML code to hide scripts from old browsers or for debugging purposes as seen in the following example.

```
<!-- <p>This paragraph has been commented out.</p> -->

<!-- The paragraph below will be displayed in the browser -->
<p>This paragraph will be displayed in the browser.</p>
```

Example 12

HTML Content Categories

In HTML all the way up to HTML 4.01 had block-level and inline-level elements. In HTML5 there are content categories and each element in HTML5 falls into none or more categories that group HTML elements with similar characteristics together. The following HTML5 content categories are listed below.

- Metadata Content

- Flow Content

- Sectioning Content

- Heading Content

- Phrasing Content

- Embedded Content

- Interactive Content

Some HTML elements also fall into other content categories which include the palpable content category, form-associated content category, script-supporting elements category, and the transparent content models. But I will not explain those categories I will only explain the main content categories I listed earlier.

Metadata Content

HTML elements associated with the metadata content category modify the presentation or the behavior of the rest of the document, that link to other documents or that conveys other out of band information.

HTML elements associated with the metadata content category are the `<base>` , `<link>` , `<meta>` , `<noscript>` , `<script>` , `<style>` , `<template>` and `<title>` elements.

Flow Content

Most HTML elements associated with the flow content category are used in the body of documents and applications usually contain text.

HTML elements associated with the flow content category are the `<a>` , `<abbr>` , `<address>` , `<area>` element only if it is a descendant of a `<map>` element, `<article>` , `<aside>` , `<audio>` , `<b>` , `<bdo>` , `<bdi>` , `<blockquote>` , `<br>` , `<button>` , `<canvas>` , `<cite>` , `<code>` , `<data>` , `<datalist>` , `<del>` , `<details>` , `<dfn>` , `<dialog>` , `<div>` , `<dl>` , `<em>` , `<embed>` , `<fieldset>` , `<figure>` , `<footer>` , `<form>` , `<h1>` , `<h2>` , `<h3>` , `<h4>` , `<h5>` , `<h6>` , `<header>` , `<hgroup>` , `<hr>` , `<i>` , `<iframe>` , `<img>` , `<input>` , `<ins>` , `<kbd>` , `<label>` , `<link>` element only if the `itemprop` attribute is present or if the `rel` attribute is present and only contains keywords that are allowed in the `<body>` element, `<main>` element only if its a hierarchically correct `<main>` element in which its ancestor elements are limited to only the `<html>` , `<body>` , `<div>` , or the `<form>` elements without an accessible name, and autonomous custom elements, `<map>` , `<mark>` , `<math>` , `<menu>` , `<meta>` element only if the `itemprop` attribute is present, `<meter>` , `<nav>` , `<noscript>` ,

`<object>` , `<ol>` , `<output>` , `<p>` , `<picture>` , `<pre>` , `<progress>` , `<q>` , `<ruby>` , `<s>` , `<samp>` , `<script>` , `<section>` , `<select>` , `<slot>` , `<small>` , `<span>` , `<strong>` , `<sub>` , `<sup>` , `<svg>` , `<table>` , `<template>` , `<textarea>` , `<time>` , `<u>` , `<ul>` , `<var>` , `<video>` , `<wbr>` , autonomous custom elements, and text.

Sectioning Content

HTML elements associated with the sectioning content category which defines the range of headings and footers.

HTML elements associated with the sectioning content category are the `<article>` , `<aside>` , `<nav>` and `<section>` elements.

Heading Content

HTML elements associated with the heading content category which defines the header of a section, whether definitively marked up using sectioning content elements, or absolutely defined by the heading content itself.

HTML elements associated with the heading content category are the `<h1>` , `<h2>` , `<h3>` , `<h4>` , `<h5>` , `<h6>` and `<hgroup>` elements.

Phrasing Content

HTML elements associated with the phrasing content category which defines the text as well as the elements that markup that text. Most HTML elements associated with the phrasing content category can only contain other phrasing content.

HTML elements associated with the phrasing content category are the `<a>` element if it only contains phrasing content, `<abbr>` , `<area>` element only if it is a descendant of a `<map>` element, `<audio>` , `<b>` , `<bdi>` , `<bdo>` , `<br>` , `<button>` , `<canvas>` , `<cite>` , `<code>` , `<data>` , `<datalist>` , `<del>` element if it only contains phrasing content, `<dfn>` , `<em>` , `<embed>` , `<i>` , `<iframe>` , `<img>` , `<input>` , `<ins>` element if it only contains phrasing content, `<kbd>` , `<label>` , `<link>` element if the `itemprop` attribute is present and only if it is allowed in the `<body>` element, `<map>` element if it only contains phrasing content, `<mark>` , `<math>` , `<meta>` element only if the `itemprop` attribute is present, `<meter>` , `<noscript>` , `<object>` , `<output>` , `<picture>` , `<progress>` , `<q>` , `<ruby>` , `<s>` , `<samp>` , `<script>` , `<select>` , `<slot>` , `<small>` , `<span>` , `<strong>` , `<sub>` , `<sup>` , `<svg>` , `<template>` , `<textarea>` , `<time>` , `<u>` , `<var>` , `<video>` , `<wbr>` , autonomous custom elements, and text.

Embedded Content

HTML elements associated with the embedded content category include elements that load external resources into the document, for example, images, videos, and Flash-based content.

HTML elements associated with the embedded content category are the `<audio>`, `<canvas>`, `<embed>`, `<iframe>`, `<img>`, `<math>`, `<object>`, `<svg>` and `<video>` elements.

Interactive Content

HTML elements associated with the interactive content category are specifically intended for user interaction. For example, depending on the user's browser and device, the user's interaction can be performed by using any kind of input device, such as, for example, a mouse, a keyboard, a touch screen, or voice input.

HTML elements associated with the interactive content category are the `<a>` element only if the `href` attribute is present, `<audio>` element only if the `controls` attribute is present, `<button>`, `<details>`, `<embed>`, `<iframe>`, `<img>` element only if the `usemap` attribute is present, `<input>` element only if the `type` attributes value is not set to the `hidden` state, `<label>`, `<object>` element only if the `usemap` attribute is present, `<select>`, `<textarea>` and the `<video>` element only if the `controls` attribute is present.

HTML Attributes

Now their is a little more to HTML attributes like boolean attributes and global attributes so let me go into more detail about HTML attributes. Let me first explain about boolean attributes.

HTML Boolean Attributes

Now their are some HTML attributes that are called boolean attributes. A boolean attribute when placed in an HTML element represents a true value, and when not placed in an HTML element the boolean attribute represents a false value.

The boolean attribute values "true" and "false" are not allowed. To represent a false value, the attribute has to be left out altogether. Let me show you what I mean in the following example using the boolean attribute `itemscope` which explains and gives information about the HTML elements content it contains between the opening and closing tags.

```
<div itemscope>This is a valid HTML boolean attribute.</div>
<div itemscope="">This is a valid HTML boolean attribute.</div>
<div iTEMscope="itemscope">This is a valid HTML boolean attribute.</div>
<div itemscope="iTemScoPe">This is a valid HTML boolean attribute.</div>
<div itemscope="itemscope">This is a valid HTML boolean attribute.</div>
<div itemscope=itemscope>This is a valid HTML boolean attribute.</div>
<div itemscope=itEmScOPe>This is a valid HTML boolean attribute.</div>

<div itemscope="true">This is NOT a valid HTML boolean attribute.</div>
```

Example 13

I think you get the point of what is a valid and not a valid boolean attribute from the above example.

HTML Global Attributes

HTML global attributes are attributes that can be used with all HTML elements. I will list the HTML global attributes below.

Accesskey Attribute

The `accesskey` attribute specifies a keyboard shortcut to activate or focus on the HTML element. The `accesskey` attributes value must be a single letter or number.

Here is how to code the `accesskey` attribute below.

```
<a href="https://www.ebooklingo.com" accesskey="e">eBookLingo.com</a>
```

Example 14

Now the way to access the shortcut key in the above example which will open the link in your browser varies from browser to browser and if you are using Windows or Mac. So I will only explain a few ways to do this below.

- In Mac for Chrome, Safari, Opera 15+: Control + Alt + `accesskey`

- In Mac for Firefox 57 or newer: Control + Option + `accesskey` or Control + Alt + `accesskey`

- In Windows for Firefox: Alt + Shift + `accesskey`

- In Windows for Edge, IE, Safari, Opera 15+: Alt + `accesskey`

Class Attribute

The `class` attribute assigns a class name or a space-separated list of class names to an HTML element. Multiple HTML elements can have the same class name. The `class` attribute is mostly used to point to a class in a CSS style sheet. The `class` attribute can also be used with JavaScript as well.

The `class` attributes value has a couple of rules listed below.

- The `class` attributes value must begin with a letter A-Z or a-z

- The `class` attributes value can then be followed by digits 0-9, letters A-Z or a-z, hyphens ("-"), and underscores ("_")

Here is how to code the `class` attribute with a single class name below.

```
<p class="first-name">This paragraph has a sinle class name.</p>
```

Example 15

And here is how to code the `class` attribute with multiple class names below.

```
<p class="first-name second-name">This paragraph has multiple class names.</p>
```

Example 16

Contenteditable Attribute

The `contenteditable` attribute specifies whether the content of an HTML element can be edited by the user or not. The two possible values are `true` which indicates that the HTML element is editable and `false` which specifies that the HTML element is not editable.

```
<p contenteditable="true">This is an editable paragraph.</p>
```

Example 17

Data-* Attribute

The `data-*` attribute is basically a custom attribute that is used to store custom data private to the page or application, so in other words the `data-*` attribute allows you to embed custom `data-*` attributes on all HTML elements that will exchange information to the DOM using scripts.

You should know that the `data-*` attributes name should not contain any uppercase letters and must be at least one character long after the prefix `data-` so in other words you can replace the asterisk `*` with any name you like as long as it follows the naming rules when creating your custom attribute.

After naming your custom `data-*` attribute you can then give it any value like.

On a side note custom attributes that start with the prefix `data-` will be completely ignored by the user agent.

Here is an example of the `data-*` attribute below.

```
<ul>
  <li data-age="60-70" data-place-of-origin="Earth (Dimension C-137)">Rick Sanchez</li>
  <li data-age="14" data-place-of-origin="Earth (Dimension C-137)">Morty Smith</li>
</ul>
```

Example 18

Dir Attribute

The `dir` attribute specifies the direction of the text for the content in the HTML element. The following values for the `dir` attribute are listed below.

- The `ltr` value states the direction of the text should be left-to-right the default value.

- The `rtl` value states the direction of the text should be right-to-left.

- The `auto` value lets the user agent figure out the direction of the text, based on the content.

Here is an example of the `dir` attribute below.

```
<p dir="rtl">This paragraph's text is going right-to-left.</p>
```

Example 19

Example as seen in FireFox 80.0.1 (64-bit) browser.

.This paragraphs text is going right-to-left

Draggable Attribute

The `draggable` attribute specifies whether an element is draggable or not. Perfect for the drag and drop work. The following values for the `draggable` attribute are listed below.

- The `true` value states that the element is draggable.
- The `false` value states that the element is not draggable.
- The `auto` value just uses the default behavior of the browser.

Here is an example of the `draggable` attribute below.

```
<p draggable="true">This paragraph is draggable.</p>
```

Example 20

Hidden Attribute

The `hidden` attribute indicates that an HTML element is not yet, or is no longer, relevant. The `hidden` attribute is a boolean attribute. User agents should not display HTML elements that have the `hidden` attribute present.

Here is an example of the `hidden` attribute below.

```
<p hidden>This paragraph is now hidden.</p>
```

Example 21

Id Attribute

The `id` attribute specifies a unique id for an HTML element. The `id` attributes value must be unique within the HTML document. So, in other words, multiple HTML elements in an HTML document should not have the same id value, only one HTML element is allowed. The `id` attributes value can't contain any space characters.

The `id` attribute is mostly used with CSS style sheets and JavaScript.

Here is an example of the `id` attribute below.

```
<p id="unique-id">This paragraph has a unique id.</p>
```

Example 22

Here is an example of the wrong and correct way to add `id` attributes to your HTML file below.

```
<p id="not-unique-id">This is the wrong way to add an id attribute.</p>
<p id="rot-unique-id">This is the wrong way to add an id attribute.</p>
<p id="whitespace id">This is also the wrong way to add an id attribute because it has a space.</p>

<p id="unique-id">This is the correct way to add an id attribute.</p>
<p id="another-unique-id">This is the correct way to add an id attribute.</p>
```

Example 23

Lang Attribute

The `lang` attribute specifies the language of the HTML elements content. The `lang` attributes value can be an ISO language code as its value. Typically this is a two-letter code such as `en` for English.

Here is an example of the `lang` attribute below.

```
<p lang="en">This paragraph is in English.</p>
```

Example 24

Below s a list of some possible values for the `lang` attribute.

Language	ISO Code
Abkhazian	ab
Afar	aa
Afrikaans	af
Akan	ak
Albanian	sq
Amharic	am
Arabc	ar

Language	ISO Code
Aragonese	an
Armenian	hy
Assamese	as
Avaric	av
Avestan	ae
Aymara	ay
Azerbaijani	az
Bambara	bm
Bashkir	ba
Basque	eu
Belarusian	be
Bengali (Bangla)	bn
Bihari	bh
Bislama	bi
Bosnian	bs
Breton	br
Bulgarian	bg
Burmese	my
Catalan	ca
Chamorro	ch
Chechen	ce
Chichewa, Chewa, Nyanja	ny
Chinese	zh
Chinese (Simplified)	zh-Hans
Chinese (Traditional)	zh-Hant
Chuvash	cv
Cornish	kw
Corsican	co
Cree	cr

Language	ISO Code
Croatian	hr
Czech	cs
Danish	da
Divehi, Dhivehi, Maldivian	dv
Dutch	nl
Dzongkha	dz
English	en
Esperanto	eo
Estonian	et
Ewe	ee
Faroese	fo
Fijian	fj
Finnish	fi
French	fr
Fula, Fulah, Pulaar, Pular	ff
Galician	gl
Gaelic (Scottish)	gd
Gaelic (Manx)	gv
Georgian	ka
German	de
Greek	el
Greenlandic	kl
Guarani	gn
Gujarati	gu
Haitian Creole	ht
Hausa	ha
Hebrew	he
Herero	hz
Hindi	hi
Hiri Motu	ho

Language	ISO Code
Hungarian	hu
Icelandic	is
Ido	io
Igbo	ig
Indonesian	id, in
Interlingua	ia
Interlingue	ie
Inuktitut	iu
Inupiak	ik
Irish	ga
Italian	it
Japanese	ja
Javanese	jv
Kalaallisut, Greenlandic	kl
Kannada	kn
Kanuri	kr
Kashmiri	ks
Kazakh	kk
Khmer	km
Kikuyu	ki
Kinyarwanda (Rwanda)	rw
Kirundi	rn
Kyrgyz	ky
Komi	kv
Kongo	kg
Korean	ko
Kurdish	ku
Kwanyama	kj
Lao	lo

Language	ISO Code
Latin	la
Latvian (Lettish)	lv
Limburgish (Limburger)	li
Lingala	ln
Lithuanian	lt
Luga-Katanga	lu
Luganda, Ganda	lg
Luxembourgish	lb
Manx	gv
Macedonian	mk
Malagasy	mg
Malay	ms
Malayalam	ml
Maltese	mt
Maori	mi
Marathi	mr
Marshallese	mh
Moldavian	mo
Mongolian	mn
Nauru	na
Navajo	nv
Ndonga	ng
Northern Ndebele	nd
Nepal	ne
Norwegian	no
Norwegian bokmål	nb
Norwegian nynorsk	nn
Nuosu	ii
Occitan	oc
Ojibwe	oj

Language	ISO Code
Old Church Slavonic, Old Bulgarian	cu
Oriya	or
Oromo (Afaan Oromo)	om
Ossetian	os
Pāli	pi
Pashto, Pushto	ps
Persian (Farsi)	fa
Polish	pl
Portuguese	pt
Punjabi (Eastern)	pa
Quechua	qu
Romansh	rm
Romanian	ro
Russian	ru
Sami	se
Samoan	sm
Sango	sg
Sanskrit	sa
Serbian	sr
Serbo-Croatian	sh
Sesotho	st
Setswana	tn
Shona	sn
Sichuan Yi	ii
Sindhi	sd
Sinhalese	si
Siswati	ss
Slovak	sk
Slovenian	sl

Language	ISO Code
Somali	so
Southern Ndebele	nr
Spanish	es
Sundanese	su
Swahili (Kiswahili)	sw
Swati	ss
Swedish	sv
Tagalog	tl
Tahitian	ty
Tajik	tg
Tamil	ta
Tatar	tt
Telugu	te
Thai	th
Tibetan	bo
Tigrinya	ti
Tonga	to
Tsonga	ts
Turkish	tr
Turkmen	tk
Twi	tw
Uyghur	ug
Ukrainian	uk
Urdu	ur
Uzbek	uz
Venda	ve
Vietnamese	vi
Volapük	vo
Wallon	wa
Welsh	cy

Language	ISO Code
Wolof	wo
Western Frisian	fy
Xhosa	xh
Yiddish	yi, ji
Yoruba	yo
Zhuang, Chuang	za
Zulu	zu

Spellcheck Attribute

The `spellcheck` attribute specifies whether the HTML element is to have its spelling and grammar checked for errors or not.

The text in the HTML `<textarea>` elements, the text values in the HTML `<input>` elements and the text in editable HTML elements like, for example, HTML elements that have the `contenteditable` attribute can all be spellchecked.

The `spellcheck` attribute can have two possible values.

- The value `true` which indicates that the HTML element should be, if possible, checked for spelling and grammar errors.

- The value `false` indicates that the HTML element should not be checked for spelling and grammar errors.

Here is an example of the `spellcheck` attribute below.

```
<p contenteditable="true" spellcheck="true">This paragraph can be spellchecked.</p>
<p contenteditable="true" spellcheck="false">This paragraph will not be spellchecked.</p>
```

Example 25

Style Attribute

The `style` attribute specifies an inline CSS style for an HTML element. The `style` attributes value can have one or more CSS declarations each separated by a semicolon `;` and each declaration is made up of a property and value separated by a colon `:`.

Here is an example below of the `style` attribute with one CSS declaration as its value which will display the text in blue.

```
<p style="color: blue;">This text will be displayed in blue.</p>
```

Example 26

Example as seen in FireFox 80.0.1 (64-bit) browser.

This text will be displayed in blue.

And here is an example below of the `style` attribute with two CSS declarations as its value which will display the text in blue and centered.

```
<p style="color: blue; text-align: center;">This text will be centered and displayed in blue.</p>
```

Example 27

Example as seen in FireFox 80.0.1 (64-bit) browser.

This text will be centered and displayed in blue.

Tabindex Attribute

The `tabindex` attribute indicates the tabbing order of an HTML element when the tab button is used for navigation which will bring focus to each HTML element in the tab order in the order they are specified.

The values of the `tabindex` attribute should be a positive number but negative numbers are also allowed.

- A value of `1` for the `tabindex` attribute is the start of the tab order.
- A negative number, for example, `-1` will not display the HTML element in the tab order.
- And if you don't want to set the order of an HTML element but just want to make sure your HTML element is focusable use the value `0` on all such HTML elements.
- The maximum value for the `tabindex` attribute is `32767`. If not specified, it takes the default value of `0`.

The order of focus on an HTML element depends on where the focus is on first, for example, if their is four HTML elements each with a `tabindex` attribute with the values ranging from `0` to `3`. And the focus is on the HTML element with the value of `2` for the `tabindex` attribute the next HTML element inline to be in focus will be the HTML element with the `tabindex` attribute that has a value of `3` and then `0` and then `1` and then back to `2` again.

Here is an example of the `tabindex` attribute below.

```
<p tabindex="2">This element will be second inline to be focused on.</p>
<p tabindex="0">This element will be last inline to be focused on.</p>
<p tabindex="-1">No focus for this element.</p>
<p tabindex="4">This element will be fourth inline to be focused on.</p>
<p tabindex="1">This element will be first inline to be focused on.</p>
<p tabindex="3">This element will be third inline to be focused on.</p>
```

Example 28

Title Attribute

The `title` attribute specifies extra information about the HTML element and when placing the mouse pointer over the element with the `title` attribute in it will display a tooltip to the user in most browsers.

The `title` attributes value can contain text as its value. You can also have text that spans multiple lines as the `title` attributes value.

Here is an example of the `title` attribute below.

```
<p title="This is a single line title for this paragraph">This is a paragraph with a title.</p>
<p title="This is a multiple line
title for this paragraph">This is a paragraph with a title that spans multiple lines.</p>
```

Example 29

Translate Attribute

The `translate` attribute specifies whether the content of an HTML element should be translated or not.

The `translate` attribute can have one of the following values.

- The value of `yes` will specify that the content of the HTML element should be translated.

- The value of `no` will specify that the content of the HTML element should not be translated.

Here is an example of the `translate` attribute below.

```
<p translate="no">This paragraph will not be translated.</p>
<p>This paragraph will be translated into another language.</p>
```

Example 30

HTML Text

HTML gives us the ability of formatting text like adding paragraphs, headings, quotations and more by only using HTML elements.

HTML Headings

The HTML heading elements `<h1>`, `<h2>`, `<h3>`, `<h4>`, `<h5>`, `<h6>` represent six levels of section headings and are displayed in bold text with the font size from big to small. `<h1>` represents the most important heading with the biggest font size and the `<h6>` represents the least important heading with the smallest font size.

You should only have one `<h1>` element per HTML web page.

Here is an example of the `<h1>`, `<h2>`, `<h3>`, `<h4>`, `<h5>`, `<h6>` elements below.

```
<h1>Heading Level 1 The Most Important</h1>
<h2>Heading Level 2</h2>
<h3>Heading Level 3</h3>
<h4>Heading Level 4</h4>
<h5>Heading Level 5</h5>
<h6>Heading Level 6 The Least Important</h6>
```

Example 31

Example as seen in FireFox 80.0.1 (64-bit) browser.

Heading Level 1 The Most Important

Heading Level 2

Heading Level 3

Heading Level 4

Heading Level 5

Heading Level 6 The Least Important

HTML Paragraphs

The HTML `<p>` element represents a paragraph.

Browsers will automatically add a single blank line before and after each HTML `<p>` element.

Here is an example of the HTML `<p>` element below.

```
<p>This is the first paragraph.</p>
<p>This is the second paragraph.</p>
```

Example 32

Example as seen in FireFox 80.0.1 (64-bit) browser.

This is the first paragraph.

This is the second paragraph.

HTML Bold Text

The HTML `<b>` element defines bold text which should be used to catch the reader's attention without conveying any special importance.

Here is an example of the HTML `<b>` element below.

```
<p>The following word is in <b>bold</b> text for your pleasure.</p>
```

Example 33

Example as seen in FireFox 80.0.1 (64-bit) browser.

The following word is in **bold** text for your pleasure.

HTML Italic Text

The HTML `<i>` element defines a range of text that is set off from the normal text for some reason, like for example, when indicating a word or phrase from another language.

The `<i>` element will display the enclosed text in italic.

Here is an example of the HTML `<i>` element below.

```
<p>The following word is in <i>italic</i> text for your pleasure.</p>
```

Example 34

Example as seen in FireFox 80.0.1 (64-bit) browser.

The following word is in *italic* text for your pleasure.

HTML Unarticulated Annotation Text

The HTML `<u>` element known as the unarticulated annotation element which was formerly the underline element defines a span of inline text which should be rendered in a way that indicates that it has a non-textual annotation, such as labeling or bringing attention to text that has been misspelt.

The content inside the HTML `<u>` element is typically displayed with a solid underline.

Here is an example of the HTML `<u>` element below.

```
<p>The misspelled word <u>pharoah</u> should be spelled pharaoh.</p>
```

Example 35

Example as seen in FireFox 80.0.1 (64-bit) browser.

The misspelled word <u>pharoah</u> should be spelled pharaoh.

HTML Text Abbreviation

The HTML abbreviation element `<abbr>` defines an abbreviation or an acronym. You may also use the optional `title` attribute with the `<abbr>` element which can provide an expansion or description for the abbreviation.

Here is an example of the HTML `<abbr>` element along with the optional `title` attribute below.

```
<p><abbr title="HyperText Markup Language">HTML</abbr> is the standard markup language for web pages.</p>
```

Example 36

Example as seen in FireFox 80.0.1 (64-bit) browser.

HTML is the standard markup language for web pages.

HTML Contact Information

The HTML `<address>` element indicates that the enclosed HTML provides contact information for a person or people, or for an organization.

The `<address>` elements contact information can be an email address, URL, physical address, phone number, social media handle or any other type of related contact inforamtion.

The `<address>` element will display the enclosed text in italic.

Here is an example of the HTML `<address>` element below.

```
<address>
Admin: Rick Sanchez<br>
eBookLingo Inc.<br>
www.ebooklingo.com<br>
12345 Fourth St.<br>
Corona CA. 92883<br>
USA<br><br>
555.555.5555
</address>
```

Example 37

Example as seen in FireFox 80.0.1 (64-bit) browser.

Admin: Rick Sanchez
eBookLingo Inc.
www.ebooklingo.com
12345 Fourth St.
Corona CA. 92883
USA

555.555.5555

HTML Bidirectional Text

The HTML bidirectional isolate element `<bdi>` informs the browsers bidirectional algorithm to treat the text that the `<bdi>` element contains to be formatted in a different direction from other text outside the `<bdi>` element.

The `<bdi>` element is perfect for when other languages like Arabic which is read and written from right-to-left is placed inside an English line of text which is read and written from left-to-right.

Here is an example of the HTML `<bdi>` element below.

```
<p>The name Aaron is written <bdi>هارون</bdi> in Arabic which is read from right-to-left.</p>
```

Example 38

Example as seen in FireFox 80.0.1 (64-bit) browser.

The name Aaron is written هارون in Arabic which is read from right-to-left.

HTML Bidirectional Text Override

The HTML bidirectional text override element `<bdo>` overrides the current directionality of the text, so that the text within the `<bdo>` element is rendered in a different direction.

The `<bdo>` element is used with the `dir` attribute which is required in order to specify the direction in which the text should be rendered inside the `<bdo>` element. The `dir` attributes possible values include:

- The value `ltr` indicates that the text should be displayed in the direction from left-to-right.
- The value `rtl` indicates that the text should be displayed in the direction from right-to-left.

Here is an example of the HTML `<bdo>` element along with its required `dir` attribute below.

```
<p>This paragraphs text will be displayed from left-to-right.</p>
<p><bdo dir="rtl">This paragraphs text will be displayed from right-to-left.</bdo></p>
```

Example 39

Example as seen in FireFox 80.0.1 (64-bit) browser.

This paragraphs text will be displayed from left-to-right.

.tfel-ot-thgir morf deyalpsid eb lliw txet shpargarap sihT

HTML Quoted Text

The HTML block quotation element `<blockquote>` indicates that the enclosed text is an extended quotation from another source.

Browsers usually indent the contents within the `<blockquote>` element.

You can also use the `cite` attribute with the `<blockquote>` element which specifies the source of the quotation. The value of the `cite` attribute should be a URL.

Here is an example of the HTML `<blockquote>` element below.

```
<blockquote>Work out your own salvation. Do not depend on others.</blockquote>
```

Example 40

Example as seen in FireFox 80.0.1 (64-bit) browser.

> Work out your own salvation. Do not depend on others.

And here is an example of the HTML `<blockquote>` element along with the `cite` attribute below.

```
<blockquote cite="https://www.ebooklingo.com/">I can and I will.</blockquote>
```

Example 41

Example as seen in FireFox 80.0.1 (64-bit) browser.

> I can and I will.

HTML Text Citation

The HTML citation element `<cite>` describes the title of a creative work, for example, a book, a song, a movie, a web site, a poem and so on.

The `<cite>` element is usually displayed in italics.

Here is an example of the HTML `<cite>` element below.

```
<p>Buy your next ebook from <cite>eBookLingo.com</cite> today!</p>
```

Example 42

Example as seen in FireFox 80.0.1 (64-bit) browser.

Buy your next ebook from *eBookLingo.com* today!

HTML Computer Code

The HTML code element `<code>` describes a piece of computer code like, for example, a snippet of HTML or CSS. The content inside the `<code>` element is displayed in the browsers default monospace font.

Here is an example of the HTML `<code>` element below.

```
<p>The CSS <code>color:</code> property defines the text color of an element.</p>
```

Example 43

Example as seen in FireFox 80.0.1 (64-bit) browser.

The CSS `color:` property defines the text color of an element.

HTML Deleted Text

The HTML deleted element `<del>` specifies that the text has been deleted from a document. User agents like browsers, for example, will usually strike a line through the deleted text contained within the `<del>` element.

Here is an example of the HTML `<del>` element below.

```
<p>The CSS <del>color:</del> property was deleted from your style sheet.</p>
```

Example 44

Example as seen in FireFox 80.0.1 (64-bit) browser.

The CSS ~~color:~~ property was deleted from your style sheet.

HTML Text Definition

The HTML definition element `<dfn>` specifies a term that is going to be defined within the content.

The `<dfn>` element is usually displayed in italics.

Here is an example of the HTML `<dfn>` element below.

```
<p><dfn>HTML</dfn> short for Hypertext Markup Language is used to describe the structure of web pages.</p>
```

Example 45

Example as seen in FireFox 80.0.1 (64-bit) browser.

HTML short for Hypertext Markup Language is used to describe the structure of web pages.

HTML Text Emphasis

The HTML emphasis element `<em>` specifies that the text within the `<em>` element has greater emphasis than the surrounding text outside the `<em>` element.

The `<em>` element is usually displayed in italics.

Here is an example of the HTML `<em>` element below.

```
<p>You've <em>got</em> to read this book!</p>
```

Example 46

Example as seen in FireFox 80.0.1 (64-bit) browser.

You've *got* to read this book!

HTML Inserted Text

The HTML inserted element `<ins>` specifies text that has been inserted into a document. User agents like browsers, for example, will usually underline the inserted text within the `<ins>` element.

Here is an example of the HTML `<ins>` element below.

```
<p>You've <ins>got</ins> to read this book!</p>
```

Example 47

Example as seen in FireFox 80.0.1 (64-bit) browser.

You've <u>got</u> to read this book!

HTML Keyboard Input

The HTML keyboard input element `<kbd>` defines text as user input from the keyboard. The `<kbd>` element is usually displayed in a monospace font by the user agents.

Here is an example of the HTML `<kbd>` element below.

```
<p>Press <kbd>Ctrl</kbd> + <kbd>A</kbd> on your keyboard to select all content.</p>
```

Example 48

Example as seen in FireFox 80.0.1 (64-bit) browser.

Press `Ctrl` + `A` on your keyboard to select all content.

HTML Marking Text

The HTML mark element `<mark>` specifies text that should be marked or highlighted, basicaly for reference or notaion purposes, due to its relevance in the surrounding context, for example, bringing attention to a particular part of a quotation.

The `<mark>` element usually highlights the background of the enclosing text in a different color which is usually in yellow.

Here is an example of the HTML `<mark>` element below.

```
<p>This is the <mark>mark</mark> element in action.</p>
```

Example 49

Example as seen in FireFox 80.0.1 (64-bit) browser.

This is the mark element in action.

HTML Measurements

The HTML measurement element `<meter>` specifies a scalar measurement within a known range, or a fractional value which is also known as a gauge. In other words the `<meter>` element can be used for a percentage on a gauge, a countdown, remaining disk space, tickets sold so far, voter turnout, money raised so far and so on.

The `<meter>` element also needs to be used with the `value` attribute which is required in order to specify the current numeric value of the gauge.

Here is an example of the HTML `<meter>` element along with its required `value` attribute below.

```
<p>Remaining disk space: <meter value="0.4">40%</meter> 40% is left.</p>
<p>Remaining disk space: <meter value="0.9">90%</meter> 90% is left.</p>
<p>Remaining disk space: <meter value="1">100%</meter> 100% is left.</p>
```

Example 50

Example as seen in FireFox 80.0.1 (64-bit) browser.

Remaining disk space: ▬▬▬   40% is left.

Remaining disk space: ▬▬▬▬▬   90% is left.

Remaining disk space: ▬▬▬▬▬   100% is left.

HTML Preformatted Text

The HTML preformatted element `<pre>` specifies preformatted text which will be displayed exctly as it is written, whitespace and all. Browsers will usually display the text within the `<pre>` element in a monospace font.

Here is an example of the HTML `<pre>` element below.

```
<pre>
html, body {
  color: #414141;
  font-family: "Segoe UI","Helvetica Neue",Arial,sans-serif;
  font-size: 17px;
  line-height: 1.7em;
  padding: 10px;
}
</pre>
```

Example 51

Example as seen in FireFox 80.0.1 (64-bit) browser.

```
html, body {
  color: #414141;
  font-family: "Segoe UI","Helvetica Neue",Arial,sans-serif;
  font-size: 17px;
  line-height: 1.7em;
  padding: 10px;
}
```

Showing A Progress Bar Using HTML

The HTML progress element `<progress>` displays a progress bar showing the progress towards a completion of a task or goal.

The `<progress>` element also has two attributes although not required they just make sense to include them with the `<progress>` element so I will explain about them below.

- The `max` attribute which indicates how much work the task or goal requires in total. The value should be a valid number. The default value is 1.

- The `value` attribute represents how much of the task or goal has already been completed. The value should be a valid number.

Here is an example of the HTML `<progress>` element along with the two attributes `max` and `value` below.

```
<p>Downloading progress: <progress value="11" max="100">11%</progress> for file 1.</p>
<p>Downloading progress: <progress value="81" max="100">81%</progress> for file 2.</p>
<p>Downloading progress: <progress value="92" max="100">92%</progress> for file 3.</p>
```

Example 52

Example as seen in FireFox 80.0.1 (64-bit) browser.

Downloading progress: ▐▐▌   for file 1.

Downloading progress: ▐▐▐▐▐▐▐▐▐▐▐▐▐▐▐▐▐ for file 2.

Downloading progress: ▐▐▐▐▐▐▐▐▐▐▐▐▐▐▐▐▐▐ for file 3.

HTML Quotation Text

The HTML quotation element `<q>` specifies a short quotation in which user agents like browsers normally insert quotation marks around the quotation contained inside the `<q>` element.

Here is an example of the HTML `<q>` element below.

```
<p>According to eBookLingo.com you can, <q>Buy, Sell & Promote Ebooks Today!</q></p>
```

Example 53

Example as seen in FireFox 80.0.1 (64-bit) browser.

According to eBookLingo.com you can, "Buy, Sell & Promote Ebooks Today!"

HTML Ruby Annotation Text

The HTML ruby annotation element `<ruby>` specifies a ruby annotation, which is basically a small extra text that is attached to the main text to give pronunciation guidance in a phonetic script for kanji in Chinese, Japanese and other languages. So, basically its small text that explains the meaning of the main text it sits on top of.

You will also need two more HTML elements which are the `<rp>` element and the `<rt>` element I will explain the `<rp>` element first.

- The HTML ruby fallback parenthesis `<rp>` element is used to provide parentheses for browsers that do not support the `<ruby>` element. Their should be two sets of `<rp>` elements the first set of the `<rp>` element should enclose the opening parentheses and the last set should enclose the closing parentheses that wrap the `<rt>` element that contains the annotation's text.

- The HTML ruby text `<rt>` element provides an explanation or pronunciation of an individual character in the ruby annotation.

Here is an example of the HTML `<ruby>` , `<rp>` and `<rt>` elements below.

```
<ruby>
  明 <rp>(</rp> <rt>ア</rt> <rp>)</rp>
  論 <rp>(</rp> <rt>ーロン</rt> <rp>)</rp>
  BIG <rp>(</rp> <rt>small</rt> <rp>)</rp>
</ruby>
```

Example 54

Example as seen in FireFox 80.0.1 (64-bit) browser.

ア ーロン small
明論BIG

HTML Inaccurate Text

The HTML inaccurate element `<s>` specifies text that is inaccurate or no longer correct, relevant or accurate. Browsers will usually add a line through the text contained within the `<s>` element.

Here is an example of the HTML `<s>` element below.

```
<p>Ebook Sale: $0.97 <s>Reg: $0.99</s></p>
```

Example 55

Example as seen in FireFox 80.0.1 (64-bit) browser.

Ebook Sale: $0.97 ~~Reg: $0.99~~

HTML Computer Sample Output

The HTML computer sample element `<samp>` defines some text as a sample or quoted output from another program or computing system. Browsers will usually display the content inside the `<samp>` element in a monospace font.

Here is an example of the HTML `<samp>` element below.

```
<p>The computer said <samp>go to eBookLingo.com to sell your eBook</samp> so I did.</p>
```

Example 56

Example as seen in FireFox 80.0.1 (64-bit) browser.

The computer said `go to eBookLingo.com to sell your eBook` so I did.

HTML Small Text

The HTML small element `<small>` defines smaller text like copyright text, legal text and so on. The text inside the `<small>` element will be displayed in a smaller font size.

Here is an example of the HTML `<small>` element below.

```
<p>This is some normal size text.</p>
<p><small>This is some smaller size text.</small></p>
```

Example 57

Example as seen in FireFox 80.0.1 (64-bit) browser.

This is some normal size text.

This is some smaller size text.

HTML Important Text

The HTML strong importance element `<strong>` defines text that has strong importance, seriousness, or urgency for the content within the `<strong>` element. The text inside the `<strong>` element will usually be displayed in bold by browsers.

Here is an example of the HTML `<strong>` element below.

```
<p>I have no importance <strong>but I have strong importance</strong>.</p>
```

Example 58

Example as seen in FireFox 80.0.1 (64-bit) browser.

I have no importance **but I have strong importance**

HTML Subscript Text

The HTML subscript element `<sub>` defines subscript text. The `<sub>` element will display its contents it contains half a character below the normal line of text in a smaller font.

Here is an example of the HTML `<sub>` element below.

```
<p>I need some H<sub>2</sub>O to drink.</p>
```

Example 59

Example as seen in FireFox 80.0.1 (64-bit) browser.

I need some H_2O to drink.

HTML Superscript Text

The HTML superscript element `<sup>` defines superscript text. The `<sup>` element will display its contents it contains half a character above the normal line of text in a smaller font.

Here is an example of the HTML `<sup>` element below.

```
<p>E = mc<sup>2</sup></p>
```

Example 60

Example as seen in FireFox 80.0.1 (64-bit) browser.

$E = mc^2$

HTML Hidden Content

The HTML template element `<template>` specifies a container for holding some HTML content that will be hidden from the user when the HTML file is loading.

The content within the `<template>` element can be displayed later by using something like, for example, JQuery or JavaScript.

Here is an example of the HTML `<template>` element below.

```
<button onclick="displayTemp()">Click me I DARE you!</button>


<template>
 <p><b>Why did you click me?</b></p>
</template>


<script>
function displayTemp() {
  var temp = document.getElementsByTagName("template")[0];
  var clone = temp.content.cloneNode(true);
  document.body.appendChild(clone);
}
</script>
```

Example 61

The above example will display a paragraph with the contents "Why did you click me?" every time you click the button "Click me I DARE you!".

HTML Time

The HTML time element `<time>` defines a specific period in time.

You can also use the `<time>` elements `datetime` attribute which translates the time and or date of the `<time>` elements contents into a machine-readable format.

The `datetime` attribute has two possible values `YYYY-MM-DDThh:mm:ssTZD` and `PTDHMS` I know this looks confusing I was stuck on stupid for a day or two so let me explain the `YYYY-MM-DDThh:mm:ssTZD` value first.

- `YYYY` - four digit year (e.g. `2020`)

- `MM` - two digit month (e.g. `08` for August)

- `DD` - two digit day of month (e.g. `09`) values can range from `01` through `31`)

- `T` or a space - a separator which is only required if a time is also specified

- `hh` - two digits for an hour (e.g. `23` for 11.00pm) values can range from (`00` through `23`)

- `mm` - two digits for a minute (e.g. `38`) values can range from `00` through `59`)

- `ss` - two digits for a second (e.g. `04`) values can range from `00` through `59`)

- `TZD` - Time Zone Designator (`Z` denotes Zulu, also known as Greenwich Mean Time) values can be `Z` or `+hh:mm` or `-hh:mm`)

Now let me explain the `datetime` attribute value `PTDHMS`.

- `P` - a prefix for Period

- `D` - a prefix for Days

- `H` - a prefix for Hours

- `M` - a prefix for Minutes

- `S` - a prefix for Seconds

Here are some examples of how to use the HTML `<time>` element and its `datetime` attribute below.

```
<p>On <time>2020-12-24</time> at <time>07:00</time> it began.</p>
<p>The year <time datetime="2020">2020</time>.</p>
<p>On <time datetime="2020-08">August 2020</time>.</p>
<p>On <time datetime="2020-08-24">24 August 2020</time>.</p>
<p>On <time datetime="08-24">24 August</time>.</p>
<p>On <time datetime="2020-W13">week 13 of the year 2020</time>.</p>
<p>On <time datetime="2020-08-24T07:00">24 August 2020 at 7:00 AM</time>.</p>
<p>On <time datetime="2020-08-24 07:00">24 August 2020 at 7:00 AM</time>.</p>
<p>On <time datetime="2020-08-24 07:22:11">24 August 2020 at 7:22:11 AM</time>.</p>
<!-- This one below has milliseconds .951 -->
<p>On <time datetime="2020-08-24 07:22:11.951">24 August 2020 at 7:22:11.951 AM</time>.</p>
<p>In <time datetime="P13D">13 Days</time>.</p>
<p>In <time datetime="PT1H24M">1 hour and 24 minutes</time>.</p>
```

Example 62

On 2020-12-24 at 07:00 it began.

The year 2020.

On August 2020

On 24 August 2020

On 24 August

On week 13 of the year 2020

On 24 August 2020 at 7:00 AM

On 24 August 2020 at 7:00 AM

On 24 August 2020 at 7:22:11 AM

On 24 August 2020 at 7:22:11.951 AM

In 13 Days

In 1 hour and 24 minutes

HTML Unarticulated Annotated Text

The HTML unarticulated annotation element `<u>` defines text that is unarticulated and styled differently from normal text. So, in other words for small parts of text that need to be presented differently. This could be used for misspelled words or to mark proper names which is basically a particular person, place, organization and so on.

The content within the `<u>` element will usually be displayed with an underline.

Here is an example of the HTML `<u>` element below.

```
<p>Did you <u>sea</u> the moon?</p>
```

Example 63

Example as seen in FireFox 80.0.1 (64-bit) browser.

Did you <u>sea</u> the moon?

HTML Variable Text

The HTML variable element `<var>` defines a variable in programming or in a mathematical expression. The content within the `<var>` element will usually be displayed in italics.

Here is an example of the HTML `<var>` element below.

```
<p><var>x</var> + 2 = 6, <var>x</var> is the variable in this example.</p>
```

Example 64

Example as seen in FireFox 80.0.1 (64-bit) browser.

x + 2 = 6, x is the variable in this example.

HTML Word Break Opportunities

The HTML word break opportunity element `<wbr>` defines a word break opportunity in a long string of text. The `<wbr>` element is useful for when you wish to specify word break opportunities in a long string of text or word. Otherwise it will break the text or word improperly.

Here is an example of the HTML `<wbr>` element below.

```
<div style="width: 13px;">
  <p>Whywontthisparagraphbreakitsdrivingmenuts!</p>
  <p>This<wbr>paragraph<wbr>will<wbr>break<wbr>because<wbr>I<wbr>made<wbr>it<wbr>so.</p>
</div>
```

Example 65

Example as seen in FireFox 80.0.1 (64-bit) browser.

Whywontthisparagraphbreakitsdrivingmenuts!

This

paragraph

will

break

because

I

made

it

so.

HTML Forms

HTML gives you the ability to interact with your users via HTML forms, by providing HTML elements to collect email addresses, phone numbers, names, passwords, credit card information, images, and other user submitted data.

Creating A Simple HTML Form

To create a simple HTML form we will need the `<form>`, `<label>` and `<input>` elements in order to create a simple HTML form that will accept a users first and last names. Let me quickly explain the HTML elements below starting with the `<form>` element.

- The `<form>` element creates an HTML form for users to enter and submit data.

- The `<label>` element will give a label to other HTML elements.

- The `<input>` element is used to create interactive input controls for the HTML form in order to allow the user to enter data.

In order to create our form, we will need to use two different types of `<input>` elements we achieve this by including the `<input>` elements `type` attribute.

Our first two `<input>` elements will need the `type` attribute with a value of `text` which will allow the user to enter text into the form via the `<input>` element.

And our third `<input>` element will need the `type` attribute with a value of `submit` which will display a submit button that will usually display the word "Submit" or "Submit Query" or something similar that the user can click in order to submit the data they entered into the HTML form to a server for validation.

Let me first show you how to code in the `<form>` and `<input>` elements and then I will explain the `<label>` elements placement.

Here is an example of the `<form>` and `<input>` elements below.

```
<form>
    First Name: <input type="text">
    Last Name: <input type="text">


    <input type="submit">
</form>
```

Example 66

Example as seen in FireFox 80.0.1 (64-bit) browser.

First Name: [   ] Last Name: [   ] Submit

Describe Your HTML Form Elements To Your Users

Now you can also label each `<input>` element, for example, you can associate the text first name to the `<input>` element that excepts the users first name in two different ways using the `<label>` element which I will show you how to do.

The first way is that you can wrap the `<label>` element around the text and `<input>` element like in the example below.

```
<form>
    <label>First Name: <input type="text"></label>
    <label>Last Name: <input type="text"></label>


    <input type="submit">
</form>
```

Example 67

Example as seen in FireFox 80.0.1 (64-bit) browser.

First Name: [   ] Last Name: [   ] Submit

The second way to associate the `<label>` element with the `<input>` element is by giving the `<input>` element an `id` attribute and the `<label>` element a `for` attribute. Both the `id` and `for` attributes values must match each other as in the following example.

```
<form>
 <label for="first_name">First Name:</label>
 <input type="text" id="first_name">

 <label for="last_name">Last Name:</label>
 <input type="text" id="last_name">

 <input type="submit">
</form>
```

Example 68

Example as seen in FireFox 80.0.1 (64-bit) browser.

First Name: [   ]   Last Name: [   ]   Submit

Custom Submit Button Name

You can also change the `<input>` elements submit buttons label which is usually the word "Submit" or "Submit Query" or something similar. In order to change the submit buttons label to say something other than "Submit" or "Submit Query" you will need to include the `<input>` elements `value` attribute which can have a text value.

Here is an example of the `<input>` elements `value` attribute for the submit button below.

```
<form>
 <label for="first_name">First Name:</label>
 <input type="text" id="first_name">

 <label for="last_name">Last Name:</label>
 <input type="text" id="last_name">

 <input type="submit" value="Register My Name">
</form>
```

Example 69

Example as seen in FireFox 80.0.1 (64-bit) browser.

First Name: [   ] Last Name: [   ] Register My Name

Checking Your Form For Errors

Now when the user clicks the `<input>` elements submit button and if you wish to have your HTML forms user submitted data validated for errors, for example, if the user entered a wrong password, email address, phone number, and so on. You will need to use the `<form>` elements `action` and `method` attributes to point to a script that will validate your form's data.

The `action` attribute specifies the location or in other words, the URL where the forms user entered data should be sent to when it is submitted. In our case our users submitted data should be sent to your script that will validate the forms data for errors.

The `method` attribute specifies the HTTP method to use when sending the forms data. You have two values to choose from listed below.

- The `get` value sends the data via the get method which is visible in the browsers address bar.

- The `post` value sends the data via the post method which is not visible to the user.

Here is an example of the `<form>` elements `action` and `method` attributes below.

```
<form action="https://www.ebooklingo.com/form-validation-script.php" method="post">
  <label for="first_name">First Name:</label>
  <input type="text" id="first_name">

  <label for="last_name">Last Name:</label>
  <input type="text" id="last_name">

  <input type="submit" value="Register My Name">
</form>
```

Example 70

Example as seen in FireFox 80.0.1 (64-bit) browser.

First Name: [   ] Last Name: [   ] Register My Name

HTML Push Buttons

To create an HTML push button using the `<input>` element we will need the `type` attribute with a value of `button` which will create a push button that is mostly used with JavaScript to run a script. You will also need to include the `<input>` elements `value` attribute which can have a text value.

We will also need one more attribute called the `onclick` event attribute, which will execute a script or call a function when the button is clicked.

Here is an example of the `<input>` element and its `type`, `value`, and `onclick` attributes below.

```
<form>
  <input type="button" value="Click Me To View The Website eBookLingo.com" onclick="viewEbookLingo()">
</form>

<script>
function viewEbookLingo() {
  window.open("https://www.ebooklingo.com/");
}
</script>
```

Example 71

Example as seen in FireFox 80.0.1 (64-bit) browser.

Click Me To View The Website eBookLingo.com

HTML Checkboxes

To create an HTML checkbox using the `<input>` element we will need the `type` attribute with a value of `checkbox` which will create a simple checkbox that can be selected or deselected. Browsers will usually display a checkbox as a square box. A user is allowed to select multiple checkboxes.

Here is an example of the `<input>` element and the `type` attribute to create a checkbox below.

```
<form>
  <label for="dog">Dog:</label>
  <input type="checkbox" id="dog">

  <label for="cat">Cat:</label>
  <input type="checkbox" id="cat">
</form>
```

Example 72

Example as seen in FireFox 80.0.1 (64-bit) browser.

Dog: ⌐ Cat: ⌐

HTML Color Picker

To create an HTML color picker using the `<input>` element we will need the `type` attribute with a value of `color` which will display a color picker allowing the user to pick a color either by using a visual color picker interface or by allowing the user to enter a color into a text field using the #rrggbb hexadecimal notation format. The default color value is #000000 black.

You can also change the color pickers default value by including the `<input>` elements `value` attribute which can have a text value.

Here is an example of the `<input>` element and the `type` attribute to create a color picker below.

```
<form>
  <label for="first_color">Choose Your First Color:</label>
  <input type="color" id="first_color">

  <label for="second_color">Choose Your Second Color:</label>
  <input type="color" id="second_color" value="#0000ff">
</form>
```

Example 73

Example as seen in FireFox 80.0.1 (64-bit) browser.

Choose Your First Color: ▄▄ Choose Your Second Color: ▄▄

Allow Users To Enter A Date Into Your HTML Forms

In HTML you can allow your users to enter a date into your HTML form by using the `<input>` element and the `type` attribute with a value of `date` which will display an input field that will let the user enter a date which includes the year, month, and day, either by the textbox that will validate the users submitted input or by a special date picker interface provided by the browser.

You can also set the dates default value by including the `<input>` elements `value` attribute with the date formatted as `YYYY-MM-DD` for the `value` attributes value.

Here is an example of the `<input>` element and the `type` attribute to create a date input field below.

```
<form>
 <label for="start_date">Start Date:</label>
 <input type="date" id="start_date">

 <label for="end_date">End Date:</label>
 <input type="date" id="end_date" value="2089-08-24">
</form>
```

Example 74

Example as seen in FireFox 80.0.1 (64-bit) browser.

Start Date: [   ] End Date: [2089-08-24   ]

Allow Users To Enter A Date & Time Into Your HTML Forms

In HTML you can allow your users to enter a date and time into your HTML form by using the `<input>` element and the `type` attribute with a value of `datetime-local` which will display an input field that will let the user enter a date and time which includes the year, month, and day as well as the time in hours and minutes, either by the textbox that will validate the users submitted input or by a special date and time picker interface provided by the browser.

You can also set the date and times default value by including the `<input>` elements `value` attribute with the date and time formatted as `YYYY-MM-DDThh:mm:ssTZD` for the `value` attributes value.

Here is an example of the `<input>` element and the `type` attribute to create a date and time input field below.

```
<form>
  <label for="start_date">Start Date:</label>
  <input type="datetime-local" id="start_date">

  <label for="end_date">End Date:</label>
  <input type="datetime-local" id="end_date" value="2089-08-24 07:22:11.951">
</form>
```

Example 75

Example as seen in FireFox 80.0.1 (64-bit) browser.

Start Date: [   ] End Date: [2089-08-24 07:22:11.95]

Allow Users To Enter An E-mail Address Into Your HTML Forms

In HTML you can allow your users to enter an e-mail address into your HTML form by using the `<input>` element and the `type` attribute with a value of `email` which will display an input field that will let the user enter an e-mail address that will be automatically validated to ensure that it's either empty or a properly formatted e-mail address or a list of e-mail addresses before the user submits the form.

Here is an example of the `<input>` element and the `type` attribute to create an e-mail input field below.

```
<form>
  <label for="your_email">Enter Your E-mail Address:</label>
  <input type="email" id="your_email">
</form>
```

Example 76

Example as seen in FireFox 80.0.1 (64-bit) browser.

Enter Your E-mail Address: [   ]

Allow Users To Enter Multiple E-mail Addresses

You can also let users enter multiple e-mail addresses using the `<input>` elements `multiple` attribute which lets users enter multiple e-mail addresses each separated by a comma, for example, `emailone@example.com, emailtwo@example.com, emailthree@example.com`. The `multiple` attribute is a boolean attribute.

Here is an example of the `<input>` element with the `multiple` attribute to create an e-mail input field that will allow users to enter multiple e-mail addresses below.

```
<form>
  <label for="multiple_emails">Enter Multiple E-mail Addresses:</label>
  <input type="email" id="multiple_emails" multiple>
</form>
```

Example 77

Example as seen in FireFox 80.0.1 (64-bit) browser.

Enter Multiple E-mail Addresses: [   ]

Allow Users To Upload Files Using HTML Forms

In HTML you can allow your users to upload files using your HTML form by using the `<input>` element and the `type` attribute with a value of `file` which will display a browse button that will let the user select a file from their device that will upload to your server when the user submits the HTML form.

You will also need the `action` and `method` attributes that I explained earlier. You will also need one other attribute called the `enctype` attribute that requires the value of `multipart/form-data` in order to allow your users to upload a file using your HTML form.

Here is an example of the `<input>` element and the `type` attribute to create a file select field below.

```
<form action="https://www.ebooklingo.com/validation-script.php" method="post" enctype="multipart/form-data">
  <label for="single_file">Select A Single File:</label>
  <input type="file" id="single_file">
</form>
```

Example 78

Example as seen in FireFox 80.0.1 (64-bit) browser.

Select A Single File: | Choose File | No file selected

Allow Users To Upload Multiple Files

You can also let users submit multiple files using the `<input>` elements `multiple` attribute which lets users select multiple files to upload. The `multiple` attribute is a boolean attribute.

Here is an example of the `<input>` element with the `multiple` attribute to create a file select field that will allow users to upload multiple files below.

```
<form action="https://www.ebooklingo.com/validation-script.php" method="post" enctype="multipart/form-data">
  <label for="multiple_files">Select Multiple Files:</label>
  <input type="file" id="multiple_files" multiple>
</form>
```
Example 79

Example as seen in FireFox 80.0.1 (64-bit) browser.

Select Multiple Files: | Choose Files | No file selected

Hide HTML Form Information From Users

In HTML you can hide information in your HTML forms from your users by using the `<input>` element and the `type` attribute with a value of `hidden` which will create a hidden input field that will hold information, like for example, the merchants id number, order id number, the cancel URL location and so on that is not visible to the user or can not be changed by the user when the form is submitted. While the hidden input field is not viewable to the user in the web pages content the hidden input field can be viewed and edited by viewing the web pages source code.

You will also need two other attributes called the `name` and `value` attributes. The `name` attributes value will give the hidden input field a name for when the form is submitted. And the `value` attribute is the input fields hidden information itself that it holds for when the HTML form is submitted to the server.

Here is an example of the `<input>` elements `type`, `name` and `value` attributes to create the hidden input field below.

```
<form>
  <label for="first_name">First Name:</label>
  <input type="text" id="first_name">
  <input type="submit">

  <input type="hidden" name="merchant_id" value="4958dfk49">
  <input type="hidden" name="order_id" value="03i09faok39592u3545436">
</form>
```

Example 80

Example as seen in FireFox 80.0.1 (64-bit) browser.

First Name: [   ] Submit

Adding An Image For Your Submit Button

In HTML you can have an image as your submit button using the `<input>` element and the `type` attribute with a value of `image` which will create the image submit button.

You will also need two other attributes called the `src` and `alt` attributes. The `src` attribute's value will be the location of the image to replace the submit button. And the `alt` attribute will display some text if the image can't be displayed for some reason.

Here is an example of the `<input>` elements `type`, `src` and `alt` attributes to create an image submit button below.

```
<form>
  <label for="first_name">First Name:</label>
  <input type="text" id="first_name">

  <input type="image" src="https://www.ebooklingo.com/images/submit.png" alt="Submit">
</form>
```

Example 81

Example as seen in FireFox 80.0.1 (64-bit) browser.

First Name: [   ] submit

Allow Users To Enter A Month And A Year Into Your HTML Forms

In HTML you can allow your users to enter a month and year into your HTML form by using the `<input>` element and the `type` attribute with a value of `month` which will display an input field that will let the user enter a month and year, either by the textbox that will validate the users submitted input or by a special month and year picker interface provided by the browser.

You can also set the month and years default value by including the `<input>` elements `value` attribute with the month and year formatted as `YYYY-MM` for the `value` attributes value.

Here is an example of the `<input>` element and the `type` attribute to create a month and year input field below.

```
<form>
  <label for="start_date">Start Date:</label>
  <input type="month" id="start_date">


  <label for="end_date">End Date:</label>
  <input type="month" id="end_date" value="2089-08">
</form>
```

Example 32

Example as seen in FireFox 80.0.1 (64-bit) browser.

Start Date: [   ] End Date: [2089-08   ]

Allow Users To Enter A Number Into Your HTML Forms

In HTML you can allow your users to enter a number into your HTML form by using the `<input>` element and the `type` attribute with a value of `number` which will display the number input field that will let the user enter a number, either by the textbox that will validate the users submitted input or by up and down arrows provided by the browser that will let the user increase or decrease the value using their mouse or fingertips.

You can also set the number to a default value by including the `<input>` elements `value` attribute which can be any floating-point number.

Here is an example of the `<input>` element and the `type` attribute to create the number input field below.

```
<form>
  <label for="apples">How Many Apples:</label>
  <input type="number" id="apples">

  <label for="oranges">How Many Oranges:</label>
  <input type="number" id="oranges" value="24">
</form>
```

Example 83

Example as seen in FireFox 80.0.1 (64-bit) browser.

How Many Apples: [   ] How Many Oranges: [24   ]

Limit The Number Value A User Can Enter

In HTML you can also limit the number a user can enter into the number input field by using the `<input>` elements `min` and `max` attributes. The `min` attribute specifies the minimum value a user can enter. And the `max` attribute specifies the maximum value a user can enter.

Here is an example of the `<input>` elements `min` and `max` attributes to limit the number value a user can enter into the number input field below.

```
<form>
  <label for="apples">How Many Apples:</label>
  <input type="number" id="apples" min="2" max="24">
</form>
```

Example 84

Example as seen in FireFox 80.0.1 (64-bit) browser.

How Many Apples: [   ]

Allow Users To Enter A Password Into Your HTML Forms

In HTML you can allow your users to enter a password into your HTML form by using the `<input>`

element and the `type` attribute with a value of `password` which will display the password input field that will let the user securely enter a password by hiding the text that is typed into the password field with asterisks "*" or bullets "•" that cannot be read on-screen. This does not encrypt the information you enter it only hides it on screen.

Here is an example of the `<input>` element and the `type` attribute to create the password input field below.

```
<form>
 <label for="secret_password">Password:</label>
 <input type="password" id="secret_password">
</form>
```

Example E5

Example as seen in FireFox 80.0.1 (64-bit) browser.

Password: ••••••••

Add Radio Buttons To Your HTML Forms

In HTML you can give your users the choice to select only one option from a group of options by using the `<input>` element and the `type` attribute with a value of `radio` which will display a radio button that will give the user the choice to select that current option that the radio button represents.

You will also need to create a few more radio buttons to create a group of options and each `<input>` element within the same group will need the `name` attribute with the same text value.

You will also need to include the `<input>` elements `value` attribute which can have a text value that will identify which radio button is selected within the group.

Here is an example of the `<input>` element and the `type` , `name` and `value` attributes to create a radio button below.

```
<form>
  <p>Favorite Fruit:</p>
  <input type="radio" id="apple" name="favorite_fruit" value="Apples">
  <label for="apple">Apples</label><br>
  <input type="radio" id="oranges" name="favorite_fruit" value="Oranges">
  <label for="oranges">Oranges</label>

  <p>Favorite Drink:</p>
  <input type="radio" id="beer" name="favorite_drink" value="Beer">
  <label for="beer">Beer</label><br>
  <input type="radio" id="water" name="favorite_drink" value="Water">
  <label for="water">Water</label><br>
  <input type="radio" id="juice" name="favorite_drink" value="Juice Box">
  <label for="juice">Juice Box</label>
</form>
```

Example 86

Example as seen in FireFox 80.0.1 (64-bit) browser.

Favorite Fruit:

- Apples
- Oranges

Favorite Drink:

- Beer
- Water
- Juice Box

How To Add A Number Range Slider To Your HTML Forms

In HTML you can add a number range slider to your HTML form by using the `<input>` element and the `type` attribute with a value of `range` which will display a number slider interface provided by the browser that will allow a user to move the slider to the desired number. The default value for the number range input slider is `100` .

You can also change the default value for the number range slider by including the <input> elements value attribute which can be any floating-point number.

Here is an example of the <input> element and the type attribute to create the number range slider below.

```
<form>
  <label for="volume_setting">Volume:</label>
  <input type="range" id="volume_setting">

  <label for="bass_setting">Bass:</label>
  <input type="range" id="bass_setting" value="81">
</form>
```

Example 87

Example as seen in FireFox 80.0.1 (64-bit) browser.

Volume:  Bass: 

Limit The Sliders Number Range

In HTML you can also limit the sliders range by using the <input> elements min and max attributes. The min attribute specifies the minimum value a user can enter. The default value for the min attribute is 0. And the max attribute specifies the maximum value a user can enter. The default value for the max attribute is 100

Here is an example of the <input> elements min and max attributes to limit the sliders range below.

```
<form>
  <label for="volume_setting">Volume:</label>
  <input type="range" id="volume_setting" min="2" max="824">
</form>
```

Example 88

Example as seen in FireFox 80.0.1 (64-bit) browser.

Volume: 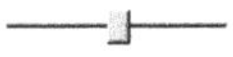

How To Add A Reset Button To Your HTML Forms

In HTML you can add a reset button to your HTML form by using the `<input>` element and the `type` attribute with a value of `reset` which will display a reset button which when pressed will reset all the forms values to their default values.

Here is an example of the `<input>` element and the `type` attribute to create the reset button below.

```
<form>
  <label for="user_id">User ID:</label>
  <input type="text" id="user_id">

  <input type="reset">
</form>
```

Example 89

Example as seen in FireFox 80.0.1 (64-bit) browser.

User ID: [   ] Reset

Allow Users To Search Your Website Using HTML Forms

In HTML you can add a search field also known as a search box to your HTML form by using the `<input>` element and the `type` attribute with a value of `search` which will display a search field for entering search strings, like for example, a Google search box, which is like a text field.

Here is an example of the `<input>` element and the `type` attribute to create a search box below.

```
<form>
  <label for="site_search">Site Search:</label>
  <input type="search" id="site_search" name="site_search">

  <input type="submit">
</form>
```

Example 90

Example as seen in FireFox 80.0.1 (64-bit) browser.

Site Search: [   ] Submit

Allow Users To Enter A Telephone Number Into Your HTML Forms

In HTML you can allow your users to enter a telephone number into your HTML form by using the `<input>` element and the `type` attribute with a value of `tel` which will display a telephone field for entering a telephone number.

Here is an example of the `<input>` element and the `type` attribute to create a telephone field below.

```
<form>
  <label for="phone">Phone Number:</label>
  <input type="tel" id="phone">
</form>
```

Example 91

Example as seen in FireFox 80.0.1 (64-bit) browser.

Phone Number: [   ]

Allow Users To Enter A Time Into Your HTML Forms

In HTML you can allow your users to enter a time into your HTML form by using the `<input>` element and the `type` attribute with a value of `time` which will display a time field for entering a time that will allow hours and minutes and optionally seconds to be entered.

Here is an example of the `<input>` element and the `type` attribute to create a time field below.

```
<form>
  <label for="time_entered">Enter A Time:</label>
  <input type="time" id="time_entered">
</form>
```

Example 92

Example as seen in FireFox 80.0.1 (64-bit) browser.

Enter A Time: [   ]

Allow Users To Enter A URL Into Your HTML Forms

In HTML you can allow your users to enter a URL into your HTML form by using the `<input>` element and the `type` attribute with a value of `url` which will display a URL field for entering an address to a web page, for example, `https://www.ebooklingo.com/`. The `<input>` elements value will be automatically validated before the form can be submitted.

Here is an example of the `<input>` element and the `type` attribute to create a URL field below.

```
<form>
 <label for="website">Enter Your Websites URL:</label>
 <input type="url" id="website">
</form>
```

Example 93

Example as seen in FireFox 80.0.1 (64-bit) browser.

Enter Your Websites URL: [   ]

Allow Users To Enter The Week And Year Into Your HTML Forms

In HTML you can allow your users to enter the week and the year into your HTML form by using the `<input>` element and the `type` attribute with a value of `week` which will display a week and year field for entering the week and year which when submitted will be formatted as follows `YYYY-WWW`. The `YYYY` represents the year, for example, `2020`. And `WWW` represents the week which can have a value of 1 to 53 and will be formatted as follows `W01` which means week one. So, if the `<input>` elements submitted value is `2020-W35` the value would represent Monday, August 24 – Sunday, August 30, 2020.

Here is an example of the `<input>` element and the `type` attribute to create a week and year field below.

```
<form>
 <label for="select_week">Select A Week:</label>
 <input type="week" id="select_week">
</form>
```

Example 94

Select A Week: [▾]

Allow Users To Enter Multiple Lines Of Text Into Your HTML Forms

In HTML you can allow your users to enter multiple lines of text into your HTML form by using the `<textarea>` element which creates a multi-line text control that can be resized by the user. The `<textarea>` element is useful for when you want your users to enter comments, feedback, reviews, and so on.

Here is an example of the `<textarea>` element to create a multi-line text control below.

```
<form>
  <label for="comment">Leave A Comment:</label>
  <textarea id="comment">Buy, Sell & Promote Ebooks Today At eBookLingo.com</textarea>
</form>
```

Example 95

Example as seen in FireFox 80.0.1 (64-bit) browser.

Leave A Comment: [Buy, Sell & Promote Ebooks Today At]

How To Add Height & Width To Your Textarea Element

You can also add height and width to the `<textarea>` element using the following attributes.

- The `rows` attribute adds height to the `<textarea>` element. The `rows` attributes value can be any number.

- The `cols` attribute adds width to the `<textarea>` element. The `cols` attributes value can be any number.

Here is an example of the `<textarea>` elements `rows` and `cols` attributes below.

```
<form>
 <label for="comment">Leave A Comment:</label>
 <textarea id="comment" rows="8" cols="81">Buy, Sell & Promote Ebooks Today At eBookLingo.com</textarea>
</form>
```

Example 96

Example as seen in FireFox 80.0.1 (64-bit) browser.

Leave A Comment:

Buy, Sell & Promote Ebooks Today At eBookLingo.com

Limit The Number Of Characters A User Can Enter

You can also limit the number of characters a user can enter into `<textarea>` element using the following attributes.

- The `minlength` attribute specifies the minimum number of characters a user is required to enter into the `<textarea>` element. The `minlength` attributes value can be any number.

- The `maxlength` attribute specifies the maximum number of characters a user can enter into the `<textarea>` element. The `maxlength` attributes value can be any number.

Here is an example of the `<textarea>` elements `minlength` and `maxlength` attributes below.

```
<form>
 <label for="comment">Leave A Comment:</label>
 <textarea id="comment" minlength="2" maxlength="4"></textarea>

 <input type="submit">
</form>
```

Example 97

Example as seen in FireFox 80.0.1 (64-bit) browser.

Leave A Comment: [ ] Submit

How To Add A Clickable Button To Your HTML Forms

In HTML you can add a clickable button to your HTML form by using the `<button>` element and the `type` attribute which can have one of three values listed below.

- The `submit` value will display a submit button that the user can click in order to submit the data they entered into the HTML form to a server for validation.

- The `reset` value will display a reset button which when pressed will reset all the form's values to their default values.

- The `button` value will create a push button that is mostly used with JavaScript to run a script.

The `<button>` element is much easier to style than the `<input>` element. You can add text and other HTML elements like the `<img>` and `<i>` elements along with other elements within the `<button>` element.

Here is an example of the `<button>` element and the `type` attribute with all its values below.

```
<form>
  <label for="user_id">User ID:</label>
  <input type="text" id="user_id">

  <button type="submit">Add User ID</button>
  <button type="reset">Reset User ID</button>
  <button type="button" onclick="viewEbookLingo()"><b>Go Back To eBookLingo.com</b></button>
</form>

<script>
function viewEbookLingo() {
  window.open("https://www.ebooklingo.com/");
}
</script>
```

Example 98

User ID: [＿＿＿＿＿＿＿＿] [Add User ID] [Reset User ID] **Go Back To eBookLingo.com**

How To Add A Drop Down List To Your HTML Forms

To add a drop down list to your HTML form you will need to use the `<select>` element which creates a menu that will list the options available to choose from. You will also need the `<select>` elements `name` attribute.

- The `name` attributes value will give the drop down list a name for when the form is submitted.

You will also need the `<option>` element that will define a menu item that is listed in the `<select>` element. The `<option>` elements are nested inside the `<select>` element. You will also need the `<option>` elements `value` attribute.

- The `value` attributes value will give the menu item a name that represents the `<option>` element for when the form is submitted.

Here is an example of the `<select>` and `<option>` elements with the `name` and `value` attributes to create the drop down list below.

```
<form>
  <label for="characters">Choose Your Favorite Character:</label>
  <select id="characters" name="favorite_characters">
   <option value="Rick">Rick Sanchez</option>
   <option value="Morty">Morty Smith</option>
   <option value="Jerry">Jerry Smith</option>
   <option value="Summer">Summer Smith</option>
   <option value="Beth">Beth Smith</option>
  </select>
</form>
```

Example 99

Example as seen in FireFox 80.0.1 (64-bit) browser.

Choose Your Favorite Character: [Rick Sanchez ▾]

Group Related Menu List Options In A Drop Down List

You can also group related menu list options using the `<optgroup>` element which is placed inside the `<select>` element. You will also need to use the `<optgroup>` elements `label` attribute which will give a name to the `<optgroup>` element.

Here is an example of the `<optgroup>` element and its `label` attribute below.

```
<form>
  <label for="characters">Choose Your Favorite Character:</label>
  <select id="characters" name="favorite_characters">
   <optgroup label="Main Characters">
    <option value="Rick">Rick Sanchez</option>
    <option value="Morty">Morty Smith</option>
    <option value="Jerry">Jerry Smith</option>
    <option value="Summer">Summer Smith</option>
    <option value="Beth">Beth Smith</option>
   </optgroup>

   <optgroup label="Secondary Characters">
    <option value="Meeseeks">Mr. Meeseeks</option>
    <option value="Doofus">Doofus Rick</option>
    <option value="Poopybutthole">Mr. Poopybutthole</option>
    <option value="President">President Morty</option>
    <option value="Squanch">Squanchy</option>
   </optgroup>
  </select>
</form>
```

Example 100

Example as seen in FireFox 80.0.1 (64-bit) browser.

Main Characters
Rick Sanchez
Morty Smith
Jerry Smith
Summer Smith
Beth Smith
Secondary Characters
Mr. Meeseeks
Doofus Rick
Mr. Poopybutthole
President Morty
Squanchy

Choose Your Favorite Character:

Preselect A Menu List Option In A Drop Down List

You can also preselect a menu list option using the `<option>` elements `selected` attribute which will make the `<option>` element its present in the default `<option>` that will be displayed first in the list. The `selected` attribute is a boolean attribute.

Here is an example of the `<option>` element and its `selected` attribute below. The Mr. Meeseeks option should now be the default option to be displayed first in the list.

```
<form>
 <label for="characters">Choose Your Favorite Character:</label>
 <select id="characters" name="favorite_characters">
  <optgroup label="Main Characters">
   <option value="Rick">Rick Sanchez</option>
   <option value="Morty">Morty Smith</option>
   <option value="Jerry">Jerry Smith</option>
   <option value="Summer">Summer Smith</option>
   <option value="Beth">Beth Smith</option>
  </optgroup>

  <optgroup label="Secondary Characters">
   <option value="Meeseeks" selected>Mr. Meeseeks</option>
   <option value="Doofus">Doofus Rick</option>
   <option value="Poopybutthole">Mr. Poopybutthole</option>
   <option value="President">President Morty</option>
   <option value="Squanch">Squanchy</option>
  </optgroup>
 </select>
</form>
```

Example 101

Example as seen in FireFox 80.0.1 (64-bit) browser.

Choose Your Favorite Character: Mr. Meeseeks ▾

Group Related Elements In Your HTML Forms

In HTML you can group related content using the `<fieldset>` element which groups related content in HTML forms. The `<fieldset>` element will draw a border surrounding the contents. You will also need the `<legend>` element which will give the content grouped by the `<fieldset>` element a caption.

Below is an example of the `<fieldset>` and `<legend>` elements to group related content and to give it a capt on.

```
<form>
 <fieldset>
  <legend>Favorite Fruit</legend>
  <input type="radio" id="apple" name="favorite_fruit" value="Apples">
  <label for="apple">Apples</label><br>
  <input type="radio" id="oranges" name="favorite_fruit" value="Oranges">
  <label for="oranges">Oranges</label>
 </fieldset>

 <fieldset>
  <legend>Favorite Character</legend>
  <select id="characters" name="favorite_characters">
   <optgroup label="Main Characters">
    <option value="Rick">Rick Sanchez</option>
    <option value="Morty">Morty Smith</option>
    <option value="Jerry">Jerry Smith</option>
    <option value="Summer">Summer Smith</option>
    <option value="Beth">Beth Smith</option>
   </optgroup>

   <optgroup label="Secondary Characters">
    <option value="Meeseeks" selected>Mr. Meeseeks</option>
    <option value="Doofus">Doofus Rick</option>
    <option value="Poopybutthole">Mr. Poopybutthole</option>
    <option value="President">President Morty</option>
    <option value="Squanch">Squanchy</option>
   </optgroup>
  </select>
 </fieldset>
</form>
```

Example 102

Example as seen in FireFox 80.0.1 (64-bit) browser.

```
┌─Favorite Fruit────────────────────────────────────────┐
│                                                        │
│   ⊙  Apples                                            │
│                                                        │
│   ⊙  Oranges                                           │
│                                                        │
└────────────────────────────────────────────────────────┘
┌─Favorite Character────────────────────────────────────┐
│                                                        │
│  Mr. Meeseeks                  ⌄                       │
│                                                        │
└────────────────────────────────────────────────────────┘
```

How To Add An Autocomplete Drop Down List To Your HTML Forms

In HTML you can add an autocomplete drop down list to your HTML forms `<input>` element by using the `<datalist>` element which creates a list of suggested options available to choose from, for example, when you do a search your search engine will offer you some suggested options to choose from, you will also need to include the `<datalist>` elements `id` attribute.

Another attribute you will need is the `<input>` elements `list` attribute and its value must be the same as the `id` attributes value for the `<datalist>` element in order to display the list of suggestions specified for that `<input>` element.

Below is an example of the `<datalist>` and `<input>` elements along with the `id` and `list` attributes to create the autocomplete drop down list of predefined suggested options.

```
<form>
 <label for="choose_character">Choose Your Favorite Character:</label>
 <input list="characters" id="choose_character" name="favorite_character">
 <datalist id="characters">
  <option value="Rick">Rick Sanchez</option>
  <option value="Morty">Morty Smith</option>
  <option value="Jerry">Jerry Smith</option>
  <option value="Summer">Summer Smith</option>
  <option value="Beth">Beth Smith</option>
 </datalist>
</form>
```

Example 103

Example as seen in FireFox 80.0.1 (64-bit) browser.

Choose Your Favorite Character: [   ]

Display A Calculation Or Result From An Application Or User In Your HTML Forms

In HTML you can display the output result from a user or a calculation from an app into your HTML forms by using the `<output>` element which displays the result of a user or a calculation from an app or web site. You will also need to include the `<output>` elements `for` attribute which points to the `id` attributes value of the HTML element or elements that are used to make the calculation. If their is multiple ids that must be pointed to they must be space-separated.

In this example, we will also need the `oninput` event attribute which means that the attribute is triggered when an HTML element receives user input. In this example, we will place the `oninput` event attribute in the `<form>` element.

Below is an example of the `<output>` element along with the `id`, `for` and `oninput` attributes in order to display the calculation.

```
<form oninput="outputResult.value=parseInt(a.value)+parseInt(b.value)">
  <input type="range" id="a" name="a" value="0"> +
  <input type="number" id="b" name="b" value="0"> =
  <output name="outputResult" for="a b"></output>
</form>
```

Example #04

Example as seen in FireFox 80.0.1 (64-bit) browser.

�|——— + [0   ▲▼] =

HTML Iframes

HTML gives you the ability to display a web page inside another web page via the iframe short for inline frame is what you will learn how to do in this section.

Display Another Web Page Inside The Current Web Page Using HTML

In order to display a web page inside another web page, you will need to use the HTML `<iframe>` element which will create an inline frame that will display another document on the web page. You will also need to include the `<iframe>` elements `src` attribute which specifies the link to the document to be displayed inside the current web page.

Below is a simple example of the `<iframe>` element along with the `src` attribute in order to display a web page inside another.

```
<iframe src="https://www.ebooklingo.com/"></iframe>
```

Example 105

Example as seen in FireFox 80.0.1 (64-bit) browser.

HTML Images

Learn how HTML gives you the ability to display images on your web page in this section.

Add Images To Your Web Pages Using HTML

In order to add an image to your web page you will need to use the HTML `<img>` element which will add an image to your web page. You will also need the `<img>` elements required `src` attribute which will point to the image you want to display on your web page. You will also need the `alt` attribute which provides some alternative text for the image in case it cannot be displayed for some reason.

Below is an example of the `<img>` element along with the `src` and `alt` attributes in order to display an image on a web page.

```
<img src="./images/logo.png" alt="eBookLingo.com logo">
```

Example 106

Example as seen in FireFox 80.0.1 (64-bit) browser.

Add Links To Specific Sections Of A Single Image Using HTML

In HTML you can create an image map which is an image with many different links, for example, think of a map of the world and each country has its own link to that country. Their are two types of image maps their is the server-side image map which uses a cgi-bin and their is a client-side image map which does not need a cgi-bin, this tutorial will cover client-side image maps. In order to create our client-side image map we are going to need the following HTML elements, which include the `<img>` , `<map>` and `<area>` elements along with some of their attributes.

First, let's link to an image using the HTML `<img>` element along with its `src` and `alt` attributes but you will also need to include one more attribute called the `usemap` attribute which is going to point to the HTML `<map>` elements `name` attribute, both the `name` and `usemap` attributes values must match each other. The `usemap` attribute must include the pound sign `#` before the `usemap` attributes value. The pound sign `#` is included because the `<img>` element is treated like an anchor.

The `<map>` element which I mentioned earlier will define our image map as well as contain the `<area>` elements that will define a section of the image as a link. You will also need to include the following attributes for the `<area>` element that I will list below.

- The `shape` attribute states the shape of the area of the image to be linked also known as a hot spot. The possible values to choose from include the `circle` value which defines a circular section. The `poly` value will define a polygonal section. The `rect` value will define a rectangular section. And the `default` value will indicate the entire image.

- The `coords` attribute defines a list of comma-separated pixel coordinates for the shape to be created that will be clickable in the image map. The number of pixel coordinates and their meaning depends upon the value specified for the `shape` attribute.

Before I continue you can use the technique that I described in the tutorial **"How To Hack The Coordinates For Your Image Map Using HTML"** to get your image maps coordinates. You can find the tutorial in this section of the book.

○ If the `shape` attributes value is `circle` there will be three coordinates `x,y,r`. The `x` and `y` coordinates will define the position of the center of the circle and the `r` will define its radius. The `x` and `y` coordinates are located in the center of the circle in the image.

Now we will need to get the radius of the circle. In order to do this we will need a second set of `x,y` coordinates, which will be to the right of our circles center `x,y` coordinates. To get the second set of coordinates you will have to move the mouses cursor in a straight line from the center `x,y` coordinates to the right of the circle, so that `y` coordinate stays the same until you reach the edge of the circle.

So, now you should have two sets of `x,y` coordinates one from the center of the circle and the other from the edge on the right side of the circle. We will now have to subtract both `x` coordinates of the circle in order to get our radius. For example, lets say we have the following coordinates `61,58` which is the center of the circle and the coordinates `122,58` which is from the right edge of the circle. We then subtract both `x` coordinates 122 - 62 = `60` where the result is our radius. So, our coordinates for the circle will be `61,58,60` we will always want to keep the center of the circles coordinates and the radius result to create our value for the `coords` attribute.

○ If the `shape` attributes value is `poly` there will be `x,y` coordinates for each point that defines the polygon. Let's take the triangle in our image, for example, it has three points that we must get the coordinates for so our value for the `coords` attribute will be `385,12, 450,121, 320,121` to make the triangle a link.

- If the `shape` attributes value is `rect` you will need the coordinates from the left top corner of the rectangle image and the bottom right corner of the rectangle image. Let's take the rectangle in our image, for example, it has two points that we must get the coordinates for so our value for the `coords` attribute will be `151,49, 294,122` to make the rectangle a link.

- The `href` attribute will specify the link the user will be taken to when the image is clicked.

- The `alt` attribute will provide some alternative text for the image in case it cannot be displayed for some reason.

Below is an example of the `<img>`, `<map>` and `<area>` elements along with their attributes in order to display our client-side image map.

```
<img src="./images/shapes.png" alt="Image of Shapes" usemap="#shapes">
<map name="shapes">
  <area shape="circle" coords="61,58,60" href="https://www.ebooklingo.com/" alt="Home Link">
  <area shape="rect" coords="151,49,294,122" href="./promote-your-book" alt="Promote Your Book Link">
  <area shape="poly" coords="385,12,450,121,320,121" href="./sign-up" alt="Free Account Link">
</map>
```

Example 107

Example as seen in FireFox 80.0.1 (64-bit) browser.

How To Create A Server-SIde Image Map Using HTML

Earlier you learned how to create a client-side image map in this tutorial you will learn how to create a server-side image map. First let's link to an image using the HTML `<img>` element along with its `src` and `alt` attributes but you will also need to include one more attribute called the `ismap` attribute which defines the image as a server-side image map. The `ismap` attribute is a boolean attribute.

Next, we will need the `<a>` element and its `href` attribute. The `href` attributes value should point to the location of the image mapping program that contains the map file. Map files usually have the extension `.map`. We will now have to wrap the `<a>` element around the `<img>` element.

Now our map file will usually contain the `shape` attributes name values which include `circle`, `poly`, `rect` and `default`. You will also need each shapes coordinates and the desired URL location for each areas value. Your map file should not contain any HTML elements or attributes just plain text.

Your image map file should look somewhat like the example below, it all depends on your server.

```
# Imagemap file=ismap.map
circle 61,58,60 home.htm
rect 151,49,294,122 promote-your-book.htm
poly 385,12,450,121,320,121 sign-up.htm
default index.htm
```

Example 108

Now below is an example of the `<img>` and `<a>` elements along with their attributes in order to create our server-side image map.

```
<a href="https://www.ebooklingo.com/cgi-bin/imagemap/ismap.map">
  <img src="./images/shapes.png" alt="Image of Shapes" ismap>
</a>
```

Example 109

How To Hack The Coordinates For Your Image Map Using HTML

In order to get your images coordinates for you to create your client-side image map without using image mapping software. You will first need to add the `ismap` attribute to the `<img>` element, you will then need to place the `<img>` element inside the `<a>` element. You will then need to add the `href` attribute with a hash mark sign `#` as its value to the `<a>` element in order to create a fake link.

Below is an example of the `<img>` and `<a>` elements along with their attributes in order to create the hack to get the images coordinates.

```
<a href="#">
  <img src="./images/shapes.png" alt="Image of Shapes" ismap>
</a>
```

*Example 1*0*

Example as seen in FireFox 80.0.1 (64-bit) browser.

Now just place your mouse pointer over the desired spot on the image and look at the bottom left corner of your browser and you should see a link and the coordinates are at the end of the link, for example take the following link, `https://www.ebooklingo.com/SimplyHTML5.php#?24,22` our coordinates will be `24,22` that we can use to create our image map.

Using HTML To Draw Graphics & Animations On A Webpage Via JavaScript

In HTML you can draw graphics and animations on the fly using the HTML `<canvas>` element which is only a container for the graphics to be displayed in you will have to use a script like JavaScript to create the graphics. By default the `<canvas>` element is displayed with a width of 300px and a height of 150px and no border. You will also need to include the `id` attribute so that a script like JavaScript can find the `<canvas>` element to use. Text placed within the `<canvas>` element will be displayed in browsers that do not support the `<canvas>` element or have JavaScript turned off.

Since we will need the coordinates of the `<canvas>` element its good to know that the coordinates of the top left corner of the `<canvas>` element are `0,0` which is is the origin. Just think of the coordinates from a rectangle the left top corner of the rectangle is the beginning and the bottom right corner of the rectangle is the ending.

For this example you will also need the `<script>` element which will be used to embed some client-side JavaScript to the web page which will interact with the `<canvas>` element. The JavaScript in the following example will create three different transparent shapes that will be displayed inside the `<canvas>` element.

```
<canvas id="shapes">
This browser does not support the HTML canvas element.
</canvas>

<script>
//get the canvas id attributes value that the script should use
var c = document.getElementById("shapes");
var ctx = c.getContext("2d");
//Turn transparency on
ctx.globalAlpha = 0.2;

//create a triangle
ctx.fillStyle = "blue";
ctx.beginPath();
ctx.moveTo(10, 60);
ctx.lineTo(90, 60);
ctx.lineTo(50, 0);
ctx.closePath();
ctx.fill();

//create a rectangle
ctx.fillStyle = "green";
ctx.fillRect(50, 40, 75, 50);

//create a circle
ctx.fillStyle = "purple";
ctx.beginPath();
ctx.arc(120, 95, 32, 0, 2*Math.PI);
ctx.fill();
</script>
```

Example 111

Example as seen in FireFox 80.0.1 (64-bit) browser.

Identify Images, Illustrations, Charts & Other Self-Contained Content Using HTML

In HTML you can identify images, graphs, tables and other self-contained content in a web page using the `<figure>` element which will define the self-contained content. You can even give the self-contained content defined by the `<figure>` element an optional caption by placing the `<figcaption>` element inside the `<figure>` element.

Below is an example of the `<figure>` and `<figcaption>` elements that will identify an image as well as give it a caption.

```
<figure>
  <img src="./images/logo.png" alt="eBookLingo.com logo">
  <figcaption>The logo for eBookLingo.com</figcaption>
</figure>
```

Example 112

Example as seen in FireFox 80.0.1 (64-bit) browser.

The logo for eBookLingo.com

Display A Different Image Based On The Size Of The Browsers Window Using HTML

In HTML you can display different images based on the size of the browsers window or device by using the `<picture>` element which defines different versions of an image to target different types of browser sizes and devices, like for example, an iPad, pc, tablet and so on.

You will also need to include one or more `<source>` elements along with its `media` and `srcset` attributes. The `<source>` element will specify the alternative image to use. The `media` attribute specifies any valid media query found in CSS as its value, for example, if the `media` attributes value is `(min-width: 900px)` our alternative image will only be displayed when the browsers screen size is more than 900px wide. And the `srcset` attribute is a required attribute that specifies the URL of the alternative image to use.

Next you will need to include the required `<img>` element and its `src` and `alt` attributes to specify a default image to be displayed. The `<img>` element must be the last element within the `<picture>`

element in order for the alternative images to be displayed. If the `<img>` element is not included no images will be displayed.

Below is an example of the `<picture>` , `<source>` and `<img>` elements along with their attributes that will display a different image based on the browsers screen size. So, just adjust your browsers screen size and watch the magic happen.

```
<picture>
  <source media="(min-width: 900px)" srcset="./images/tri.png">
  <source media="(min-width: 720px)" srcset="./images/rect.png">
  <img src="./images/circle.png" alt="An image of a shape">
</picture>
```

Example 113

Example as seen in FireFox 80.0.1 (64-bit) browser.

Learn How To Draw Vector Graphics On A Web Page Using HTML

In HTML you can draw scalable vector images, create animations, and much much more using the `<svg>` element which will allow you to add SVG graphics to your web page.

Now in this tutorial we are going to display some rotated text so we will also need to include the SVG `<text>` element which creates a graphics element made up of text. We will also need to include the `<text>` elements `x` , `y` , `fill` and `transform` attributes.

- The `x` attribute describes the horizontal coordinate of the `<text>` elements position.

- The `y` attribute describes the vertical coordinate of the `<text>` elements position.

- The `fill` attribute specifies the color. The `fill` attributes color value can be a named color, a hex color, an rgb or rgba color or an hsl or hsla color.

- The `transform` attributes value can be any CSS `transform` property that lets you rotate, scale, etc., the `<text>` element.

Below is an example of the `<svg>` and `<text>` elements along with their attributes that will display the rotated text.

```
<svg>
 <text x="0" y="13" fill="#47ADE0" transform="rotate(30,20,40)">eBookLingo.com</text>
 <text x="100" y="4" fill="#22c463" transform="rotate(90,124,22)">What's Your Lingo?</text>
</svg>
```

Example 114

Example as seen in FireFox 80.0.1 (64-bit) browser.

HTML Audio & Video

Learn how HTML gives you the ability to add audio and video to your web page in this section.

How To Add A Playable Audio File To Your Web Page Using HTML

In HTML you can add a playable audio file to your web page that a user can choose to play or not by using the `<audio>` element which adds the audio content to the web page, for example, music. You will also need to include the `<audio>` elements `controls` attribute which displays the browsers default audio controls, for example, the play, volume and pause buttons. The `controls` attribute is a boolean attribute.

You will also need to include one or more `<source>` elements along with its `src` and `type` attributes. The `<source>` element will specify the audio file that is available for use. The browser will usually choose the first audio source it supports. The `src` attribute specifies the URL of the audio file that is available to be played. And the `type` attribute indicates the MIME type for the audio file that you indicated as the value for the `src` attribute. For example, `audio.mp3` will have a MIME type of `audio/mpeg` depending on the multimedia player.

Below is a list of some of the most popular audio MIME types.

Media Type	File Extension	MIME Type
Audio	.au	audio/basic
Audio	.mid	audio/mid
Audio	.rmi	audio/mid
Audio	.mp3	audio/mpeg
Audio	.mp4	audio/mp4
Audio	.ogg	audio/ogg
Audio	.wav	audio/wav

Below is an example of the `<audio>` and `<source>` elements along with their attributes to add a playable audio file to your web page.

```
<audio controls>
  <source src="./media/audio.ogg" type="audio/ogg">
  <source src="./media/audio.mp3" type="audio/mpeg">
</audio>
```

Example 115

Example as seen in FireFox 80.0.1 (64-bit) browser.

How To Add A Playable Video File To Your Web Page Using HTML

In HTML you can add a playable video or movie file to your web page that a user can choose to play or not by using the `<video>` element which adds the video content to the web page, for example, a music video, a movie clip and so on. You will also need to include the `<video>` elements `controls` attribute which displays the browsers default video controls, for example, the play, volume and pause buttons. The `controls` attribute is a boolean attribute.

You will also need to include one or more `<source>` elements along with its `src` and `type` attributes. The `<source>` element will specify the video file that is available for use. The browser will usually choose the first video source it supports. The `src` attribute specifies the URL of the video file that is available to be played. And the `type` attribute indicates the MIME type for the video file that you indicated as the value for the `src` attribute. For example, `video.mp4` will have a MIME type of `video/mp4` depending on the multimedia player.

Below is a list of some of the most popular video MIME types.

Media Type	File Extension	MIME Type
Video	.flv	video/x-flv
Video	.mp4	video/mp4
Video	.m3u8	application/x-mpegURL
Video	.ts	video/MP2T

Media Type	File Extension	MIME Type
Video	.3gp	video/3gpp
Video	.mov	video/quicktime
Video	.ogg	video/ogg
Video	.avi	video/x-msvideo
Video	.wmv	video/x-ms-wmv
Video	.webm	video/webm

Below is an example of the `<video>` and `<source>` elements along with their attributes to add a playable video or movie file to your web page.

```
<video controls>
  <source src="./media/video.mp4" type="video/mp4">
  <source src="./media/video.webm" type="video/webm">
</video>
```

Example 116

Example as seen in FireFox 80.0.1 (64-bit) browser.

How To Add Subtitles To Your Audio & Video Files Using HTML

In HTML you can add subtitles to your audio and video files by including the `<track>` element and its `src`, `kind`, `srclang` and `label` attributes and placing them inside the `<audio>` or `<video>` elements.

The `<track>` element will specify a timed text track file, for example, a subtitle or caption file for the `<audio>` and `<video>` elements.

The `src` attribute specifies the URL of the timed text track file. Timed text track files are formatted using the WebVTT format and have a `.vtt` file extension.

The `kind` attribute states the kind of data contained inside the timed text track file that will be used. The `kind` attribute excepts the following values listed below.

- The `captions` value indicates the translation of dialogue and sound effects which is best for when the sound is unavailable or not clearly audible, for example, because the user is deaf.
- The `chapters` value indicates the chapter titles which is best for when navigating through the audio or video file.
- The `descriptions` value defines a textual description of the audio or video files content which is best for blind users.
- The `metadata` value indicates that the timed track file is to be used by scripts and is not visible to the user.
- The `subtitles` value indicates that subtitles should be available for the audio or video file.

The `srclang` attribute value defines a two letter language code that specifies the language of the data for the text track file. For example, the Hindi language will be `hi`, the Japanese language will be `ja` and so on.

The `label` attribute will simply give a title to the timed text track file.

Now in the example below we are going to place the `<track>` element and its attributes inside the `<video>` element to give our video some subtitles in both English and Spanish in which the user can choose from. A captions and subtitles control should be displayed in the video controls panel.

```
<video controls>
  <source src="./media/video.mp4" type="video/mp4">
  <track src="./media/subtitles-en.vtt" kind="subtitles" srclang="en" label="English">
  <track src="./media/subtitles-es.vtt" kind="subtitles" srclang="es" label="Spanish">
</video>
```

Example 117

Display A Thumbnail Image While The Video Is Downloading Or Until Played Using HTML

Now you can display a poster image also known as a placeholder image or thumbnail image while the video is downloading or until the video is played by using the HTML `poster` attribute for the `<video>` element. The `poster` attributes value should be a URL link to the image that will be used as the thumbnail image for the `<video>` element.

Now in the example below we are going to add the `poster` attribute to the `<video>` element in order to display an image while the video is downloading and before the video is played.

```
<video controls poster="./images/square-logo.png">
  <source src="./media/video.mp4" type="video/mp4">
  <source src="./media/video.webm" type="video/webm">
</video>
```

Example 118

Example as seen in FireFox 80.0.1 (64-bit) browser.

HTML Links

Learn how to link from one web page to another as well as how to download content and much more using HTML in this section.

Link To Another Web Page Using HTML

In HTML you can link from one web page to another using the `<a>` element and its `href` attribute. The `<a>` element creates the link also known as hyperlink, which is used to link from one web page to another. The `href` attribute specifies the URL link to the other web page the user will be taken to when the link is clicked.

Below is an example of the `<a>` element and its `href` attribute to create our link to the web site ebooklingo.com.

```
<a href="https://www.ebooklingo.com/">eBookLing.com</a>
```

Example 119

Example as seen in FireFox 80.0.1 (64-bit) browser.

eBookLing.com

What Are Absolute & Relative URLs?

Now when specifying a URL link to a web page you can use a relative URL or an absolute URL. I will explain each in this section.

Absolute URLs

Absolute URLs are best for when you want to link to another web site, for example, lets say we want to link to amazon.com from ebooklingo.com we will have to use an absolute link which is the full path or in other words all the information the server will need to find the web site. To specify an absolute URL you will need to include the following listed below.

- The protocol, for example, `http://` , `https://` , `ftp://` , `gopher://` , or `file://`
- The host name, for example, `www.ebooklingo.com`
- The path to the web page, for instance, `index.htm`

Below are some examples of absolute URLs.

```
https://www.ebooklingo.com/
https://www.ebooklingo.com/promote-your-book.php
https://www.ebooklingo.com/sell-your-ebook.php
```

Example 120

Below are examples of the `<a>` elements `href` attribute using absolute URL values to create some links.

```
<a href="https://www.ebooklingo.com/">Home Page</a> <br>
<a href="https://www.ebooklingo.com/promote-your-book.php">Promote Your Book</a> <br>
<a href="https://www.ebooklingo.com/sell-your-ebook.php">Sell Your Book</a>
```

Example 121

Example as seen in FireFox 80.0.1 (64-bit) browser.

Home Page

Promote Your Book

Sell Your Book

Relative URLs

Now relative URLs are best for when you are linking within your own web site and not to an outside web site. Also a relative URL will never include the `http://` , `https://` , `ftp://` , `gopher://` , or `file://` protocols.

To specify a relative URL you can use one of the following methods or a combination of the methods listed below.

```
/
./
../
another-file.htm
../../images/
../../images/logo.png
```

Example 122

Let me explain the above example in more detail.

- The single slash `/` will direct the browser to take you back to the home page of the web site no matter what page you are currently on in the same site.

- One dot and a single slash `./` will direct the browser to the current directory.

- Two dots and a single slash `../` will direct the browser to take you one directory up from the current directory.

- Just including the file name itself, for example, in our case the file name `another-file.htm` will direct the browser to the current directory.

- Two dots and a single slash repeated twice plus the folder name `../../images/` will direct the browser to go two directories up and then look for the folder which in our case is the `images` directory.

- And in the last example with two dots and a single slash repeated twice plus the folder name along with the image files name `../../images/logo.png` will direct the browser to go two directories up and then look for the folder which in our case is the `images` directory and then search for the image file which again in our case is the image file `logo.png`.

Below are some examples of relative URL values in use.

```
<a href="/">Back to the main page</a> <br>
<a href="./">This directory</a> <br>
<a href="../">Move up one directory</a> <br>
<a href="another-file.htm">Another file in this directory</a> <br>
<a href="../../images/">Images directory</a> <br>
<img src="../../images/logo.png" alt="eBookLingo.com logo">
```

Example 123

Example as seen in FireFox 80.0.1 (64-bit) browser.

Back to the main page

This directory

Move up one directory

Another file in this directory

Images directory

One last thing you should know is that folder and file names are case-sensitive in URLs. For example, the files `index.htm` and `Index.htm` are two different files. However, domain names are not case-sensitive, for example, `www.ebooklingo.com` will take you to the same exact place as `WWW.EBOOKLINGO.COM` .

How To Code A URL The Correct Way

Now when you write a URL, which is short for Uniform Resource Locator, which is a web pages address. You will need to encode non-printing characters as well as reserved and unsafe characters.

An example of a non-printing character are spaces, you will need to encode non-printing characters by using the US-ASCII URL encoding character set. You can type a space in a URL but it won't be a valid URL but it will still work. If you want a valid URL you will have to replace the space in the URL with the US-ASCII URL encoding character `%20` in order for the URL to be valid.

The example below will show you the wrong and the correct way to write a URL.

```
<a href="http://www.ebooklingo.com/search.php?search=self help ebooks">This is the wrong way</a> <br>
<a href="http://www.ebooklingo.com/search.php?search=self%20help%20ebooks">This is the correct way</a>
```

Example 124

Example as seen in FireFox 80.0.1 (64-bit) browser.

This is the wrong way

This is the correct way

Now reserved characters are characters that have a special meaning within the URL. An example of some reserved characters are the colon `:` as well as the slash `/` signs, and if you wish to include a slash that's not intended to be a separator you will have to encode the slash with the `%2f` encoding.

Now unsafe characters are characters that do not have any special meaning within the URL but may have a special meaning in the way the URL is written. An example of an unsafe character is the hash sign `#` which should always be encoded because it's used in systems to determine a URL from an anchor identifier that usually follows it.

Just to let you know any character other than a number, letter or any special character like `$-_.+!*'()` should be encoded.

You can encode any character in a URL except for the characters that have a special meaning, for example, encoding the double slashes // in an HTTP URL will cause them to be used as regular characters and not as the pathname delimiters for which they are intended for.

Below is a list of non-printing, reserved, and unsafe characters along with their URL encodings.

Character	Description	Type	ASCII URL Encoding
:	Colon	Reserved	%3a
;	Semicolon	Reserved	%3b
=	Equals Sign	Reserved	%3d
?	Question Mark	Reserved	%3f
/	Slash	Reserved	%2f
@	At Sign	Reserved	%40
&	Ampersand	Reserved	%26
	Tab	Unsafe	%09
	Space	Unsafe	%20
<	Less-Than Sign	Unsafe	%3c
>	Greater-Than Sign	Unsafe	%3e
"	Double Quotation Mark	Unsafe	%22
#	Hash Symbol	Unsafe	%23
%	Percent	Unsafe	%25
\	Backslash	Unsafe	%5c
[	Left Square Bracket	Unsafe	%5b
]	Right Square Bracket	Unsafe	%5d
^	Caret	Unsafe	%5e
`	Back Single Quotation Mark	Unsafe	%60
{	Left Curly Brace	Unsafe	%7b
}	Right Curly Brace	Unsafe	%7d
|	Vertical Bar	Unsafe	%7c
~	Tilde	Unsafe	%7e

How To Tell The Browser Where To Open A Link

In HTML you can tell a browser how it should open your linked document by using the `target` attribute and one of its reserved target name values for the `<a>` element listed below.

- The `_blank` value will tell the browser to always open the link in a new browser window.

- The `_self` value is the `<a>` elements default value which will instruct the targeted link to load in the same window or tab.

- The `_parent` value will load the targeted link into the parent window or frame containing the `_parent` value. Now if the `_parent` value is indicated in a top-level frame or window it is equal to the target name value `_self`.

- The `_top` value will open in a full browser window.

All the target reserved names begin with an underscore `_` character. You should not use an underscore as the first character for any other target name values other then the four reserved target name values, if you do the value will be ignored by all browsers.

Below are examples of the `<a>` element and its `target` attributes values to tell the browser how to open a link.

```
<a href="https://www.ebooklingo.com/" target="_blank">eBookLingo.com</a> <br>
<a href="https://www.ebooklingo.com/" target="_self">eBookLingo.com</a> <br>
<a href="https://www.ebooklingo.com/" target="_parent">eBookLingo.com</a> <br>
<a href="https://www.ebooklingo.com/" target="_top">eBookLingo.com</a>
```

Example 125

Link Within The Same Web Page Or To A Specific Section Of Another Web Page

Using HTML you can link within the same web page or to a specific section of another web page.

Jump To A Specific Section In The Same Web Page

Now in order to create an anchor within the same web page, you will have to use the `<a>` element along with the `id` attribute. The value of the anchor for the `id` attribute will be the text that will be used to internally identify the section of the web page you want to jump to. You can either use text or images that you wish to be referenced.

Once you have created the anchor you will then have to create a link for your users to click, when the link is clicked by your users it will then bring your users back to the section of the web page that contains the anchor.

In order to create the link, we will need to use the `<a>` element again this time with the `href` attribute. Now the `href` attributes value must include the hash sign `#` followed by the anchors `id` attributes value.

Below is an example of how to create the anchor as well as the link to the anchor to the section of the web page you want to jump to using the `<a>` element and its `id` and `href` attributes.

```
<a href="#anchor_to_chapter_1">Jump To Chapter 1</a>
//Some content should be between the link to the anchor and the anchor for it to anchor
<a id="anchor_to_chapter_1">Chapter 1</a>
```

Example 126

Jump To A Specific Section On A Different Web Page

Now if the anchor is located on a different web page in the same directory, you will have to include the file name of the web page followed by the hash sign `#` and the `id` attributes value. There should also be no spaces between the URL and the hash sign `#`.

I will show you what I mean with the example below.

```
<a href="anchor.htm#chapter_2">Go To Chapter 2</a>
```

Example 127

Now if the anchor is on a different web page not located in the same directory you will have to use the complete URL of the location of the web page followed by the hash sign `#` and then followed by the `id` attributes value from the anchor, as I will demonstrate in the example below.

```
<a href="https://www.ebooklingo.com/faq#q1">Which ebook format should I choose?</a>
```

Example 128

One thing you should know is that if the anchor is located at the bottom of the web page it may not be displayed at the top of the window, but somewhere towards the middle if there is not enough content to fill the browser window. Also, if your web page does not have enough content your anchors will not be usable.

Add A Downloadable Link To Your Web Page Using HTML

In HTML you can state that a links URL is to be downloaded when clicked instead of navigating to it, this is accomplished by adding the download attribute to the <a> element. You can simply just add the download attribute to the <a> element or you can give the download attribute a value that will rename the file name when downloaded.

Below is an example of the <a> element with the download attribute with and without a value to create our downloadable links.

```
<a href="../../images/logo.png" download>Download eBookLingo.com Image</a> <br>
<a href="../../images/logo.png" download="eBookLingo.com Logo">Download eBookLingo.com Image</a>
```

Example 129

Example as seen in FireFox 80.0.1 (64-bit) browser.

Download eBookLingo.com Image
Download eBookLingo.com Image

Add An Email Link To Your Web Page Using HTML

HTML also gives you a way to link to an email address, in order to do this you will need to use the <a> element and the href attribute, you will also need to place the mailto: protocol inside the href attribute which is then followed by the email address you want the email to be sent to.

When a user clicks on the mailto: link it will launch the default email program or the program your user set to handle their email.

Below is an example of how to create a mailto: link to send an email using the <a> element and the href attribute and its mailto: protocol.

```
<a href="mailto:rick@ebooklingo.com">Send Email</a>
```

Example 130

Example as seen in FireFox 80.0.1 (64-bit) browser.

Send Email

If you want to send an email to multiple recipients just use a comma `,` to separate each email address as seen in the example below.

```
<a href="mailto:rick@ebooklingo.com,morty@ebooklingo.com">Send Email</a>
```

Example 131

Example as seen in FireFox 80.0.1 (64-bit) browser.

Send Email

You can also add the `subject`, `cc`, `bcc`, and `body` fields to your email link.

- The `subject` field is for the subject line

- The `cc` field is for sending a carbon copy

- The `bcc` field is for sending a blind carbon copy

- The `body` field is for the email message

Now to add one of the field commands to the email address will require you to add just one question mark `?` at the start followed by the command and an equal sign `=` and then the value for the command, for example, `mailto:rick@ebooklingo.com?subject=Hello,%20Rick`. This is because the `mailto:` link is treated like a query string. You will then need to add an ampersand `&` between each additional field command also known as a query parameter, for example, `mailto:rick@ebooklingo.com?subject=Hello,%20Rick&body=Jerry%20SUCKS%21`.

White spaces are not allowed within the `href` attribute so you will have to replace each space with the ASCII URL encoding `%20` which represents a space.

Below is an example of the first field command which will start with a question mark `?`.

```
<a href="mailto:rick@ebooklingo.com?subject=Hello,%20Rick">Send Email</a>
```

Example 132

Example as seen in FireFox 80.0.1 (64-bit) browser.

Send Email

Now, let's add some additional field commands also known as query parameters which are separated by an ampersand `&`.

```
<a href="mailto:rick@w3.org?subject=Hello,%20Rick&bcc=beth@w3.org&body=Jerry%20SUCKS%21">Send Email</a>
```
Example 133

Example as seen in FireFox 80.0.1 (64-bit) browser.

Send Email

Add A Click To Call Link To Your Web Page Using HTML

HTML also gives you a way to create a click to call link, in order to do this you will need to use the `<a>` element and the `href` attribute, you will also need to place the `tel:` protocol inside the `href` attribute which is then followed by the phone number you want to be called. It's important to remember that you must only include the phone number with no spaces or dashes.

When a user clicks on the `tel:` link it will usually dial the number on a phone. But in a browser it will launch the default phone app and make the call or whatever steps the phone app takes when handling a click to call link.

Below is an example of how to create a `tel:` link to dial the phone number when the link is clicked using the `<a>` element and the `href` attribute and its `tel:` protocol.

```
<a href="tel:5556662422">Tel: 555.666.2422</a>
```
Example 134

Example as seen in FireFox 80.0.1 (64-bit) browser.

Tel: 555.666.2422

Add An Extension To Your Click To Call Link Using HTML

You can also add an extension to your click to call link in one of two ways by adding the letter `p` in front of the extension which will add a one-second pause or you can use the letter `w` which will wait for a dial tone. The extension number is added to the end of the phone number.

Below are examples of how to add an extension to your click to call link using the letter `p` for a one-second pause and the letter `w` to wait for a dial tone.

```
<a href="tel:5556662422p13">Tel: 555.666.2422 ext. 13</a> <br>
<a href="tel:5556662422w13">Tel: 555.666.2422 ext. 13</a>
```

Example 135

Example as seen in FireFox 80.0.1 (64-bit) browser.

Tel: 555.666.2422 ext. 13
Tel: 555.666.2422 ext. 13

Add A Country Code To Your Click To Call Link Using HTML

You can also add a country code to your click to call link by including a plus sign `+` along with the desired country code before the phone number.

In our example below I will show you how to add the country code to specify a phone number in Spain which is the number `34` and then I will list some country codes you can use when creating your click to call links.

```
<a href="tel:+345556662422">Tel: 34.555.666.2422</a>
```

Example 136

Example as seen in FireFox 80.0.1 (64-bit) browser.

Tel: 34.555.666.2422

Below is a list of some country codes you can use.

Country	Country Code	Exit Code	Trunk Prefix
Afghanistan	93	00	0
Albania	355	00	0
Algeria	213	00	0
American Samoa	1	011	1
Andorra	376	00	-

Country	Country Code	Exit Code	Trunk Prefix
Angola	244	00	-
Anguilla	1	011	1
Antigua and Barbuda	1	011	1
Argentina	54	00	0
Armenia	374	00	0
Aruba	297	00	-
Ascension	247	00	-
Australia	61	0011	0
Austria	43	00	0
Azerbaijan	994	00	0
Bahamas	1	011	1
Bahrain	973	00	-
Bangladesh	880	00	0
Barbados	1	011	1
Belarus	375	810	80
Belgium	32	00	0
Belize	501	00	-
Benin	229	00	-
Bermuda	1	011	1
Bhutan	975	00	-
Bolivia	591	00	0
Bosnia and Herzegovina	387	00	0
Botswana	267	00	-
Brazil	55	0014 - Brasil Telecom 0015 - Telefonica 0021 - Embratel 0023 - Intelig 0031 - Telmar	0
British Virgin Islands	1	011	1
Brunei	673	00	-
Bulgaria	359	00	0

Country	Country Code	Exit Code	Trunk Prefix
Burkina Faso	226	00	-
Burundi	257	00	-
Cambodia	855	001, 007, 008	0
Cameroon	237	00	-
Canada	1	011	1
Cape Verde	238	00	-
Cayman Islands	1	011	1
Central African Republic	236	00	-
Chad	235	00	-
Chile	56	1230 - Entel 1200 - Globus 1220 - Manquehue 1810 - Movistar 1690 - Netline 1710 - Telmex	-
China	86	00	0
Colombia	57	005 - UNE EPM 007 - ETB 009 - Movistar 00414 - Tigo 00468 - Avantel 00456 - Claro Fixed 00444 - Claro Mobile	0
Comoros	269	00	-
Congo	242	00	-
Cook Islands	682	00	-
Costa Rica	506	00	-
Croatia	385	00	0
Cuba	53	119	0
Curacao	599	00	0
Cyprus	357	00	-

Country	Country Code	Exit Code	Trunk Prefix
Czech Republic	420	00	-
Democratic Republic of Congo	243	00	0
Denmark	45	00	-
Diego Garcia	246	00	-
Djibouti	253	00	-
Dominica	1	011	1
Dominican Republic	1	011	1
East Timor	670	00	-
Ecuador	593	00	0
Egypt	20	00	0
El Salvador	503	00	-
Equatorial Guinea	240	00	-
Eritrea	291	00	0
Estonia	372	00	-
Ethiopia	251	00	0
Falkland (Malvinas) Islands	500	00	-
Faroe Islands	298	00	-
Fiji	679	00	-
Finland	358	00, 990, 994, 999	0
France	33	00	0
French Guiana	594	00	0
French Polynesia	689	00	-
Gabon	241	00	0
Gambia	220	00	-
Georgia	995	00	0
Germany	49	00	0
Ghana	233	00	0
Gibraltar	350	00	-

Country	Country Code	Exit Code	Trunk Prefix
Greece	30	00	-
Greenland	299	00	-
Grenada	1	011	1
Guadeloupe	590	00	0
Guam	1	011	1
Guatemala	502	00	-
Guinea	224	00	-
Guinea-Bissau	245	00	-
Guyana	592	001	-
Haiti	509	00	-
Honduras	504	00	-
Hong Kong	852	001	-
Hungary	36	00	06
Iceland	354	00	-
India	91	00	0
Indonesia	62	001, 008 - Indosat 007 - Telkom 009 - Bakrie Telecom	0
Inmarsat Satellite	870	00	-
Iran	98	00	0
Iraq	964	00	-
Ireland	353	00	0
Iridium Satellite	8816/8817	00	-
Israel	972	00, 012, 013, 014, 018	0
Italy	39	00	-
Ivory Coast	225	00	-
Jamaica	1	011	1
Japan	81	010	0
Jordan	962	00	0

Country	Country Code	Exit Code	Trunk Prefix
Kazakhstan	7	8 - wait for dial tone - 10	8
Kenya	254	000 (006 and 007 to Uganda and Tanzania)	0
Kiribati	686	00	-
Kosovo	383	00	0
Kuwait	965	00	-
Kyrgyzstan	996	00	0
Laos	856	00	0
Latvia	371	00	-
Lebanon	961	00	0
Lesotho	266	00	-
Liberia	231	00	-
Libya	218	00	0
Liechtenstein	423	00	-
Lithuania	370	00	8
Luxembourg	352	00	-
Macau	853	00	-
Macedonia	389	00	0
Madagascar	261	00	0
Malawi	265	00	-
Malaysia	60	00	0
Maldives	960	00	-
Mali	223	00	-
Malta	356	00	-
Marshall Islands	692	011	1
Martinique	596	00	0
Mauritania	222	00	-
Mauritius	230	00	-
Mayotte	262	00	0

Country	Country Code	Exit Code	Trunk Prefix
Mexico	52	00	-
Micronesia	691	011	1
Moldova	373	00	0
Monaco	377	00	-
Mongolia	976	001	0
Montenegro	382	00	0
Montserrat	1	011	1
Morocco	212	00	0
Mozambique	258	00	-
Myanmar	95	00	0
Namibia	264	00	0
Nauru	674	00	-
Nepal	977	00	0
Netherlands	31	00	0
Netherlands Antilles	599	00	-
New Caledonia	687	00	-
New Zealand	64	00	0
Nicaragua	505	00	-
Niger	227	00	-
Nigeria	234	009	0
Niue	683	00	-
Norfolk Island	672	00	-
North Korea	850	99	-
Northern Marianas	1	011	1
Norway	47	00	-
Oman	968	00	-
Pakistan	92	00	0
Palau	680	011	-
Palestine	970	00	0
Panama	507	00	-

Country	Country Code	Exit Code	Trunk Prefix
Papua New Guinea	675	00	-
Paraguay	595	00	0
Peru	51	00	0
Philippines	63	00	0
Poland	48	00	-
Portugal	351	00	-
Puerto Rico	1	011	1
Qatar	974	00	-
Reunion	262	00	0
Romania	40	00	0
Russian Federation	7	8 - wait for dial tone - 10	8
Rwanda	250	00	-
Saint Helena	290	00	-
Saint Kitts and Nevis	1	011	1
Saint Lucia	1	011	1
Saint Barthelemy	590	00	0
Saint Martin (French part)	590	00	0
Saint Pierre and Miquelon	508	00	-
Saint Vincent and the Grenadines	1	011	1
Samoa	685	0	-
San Marino	378	00	-
Sao Tome and Principe	239	00	-
Saudi Arabia	966	00	0
Senegal	221	00	-
Serbia	381	00	0
Seychelles	248	00	-
Sierra Leone	232	00	0

Country	Country Code	Exit Code	Trunk Prefix
Singapore	65	001, 008	-
Sint Maarten	1	00	1
Slovakia	421	00	0
Slovenia	386	00	0
Solomon Islands	677	00	-
Somalia	252	00	-
South Africa	27	00	0
South Korea	82	001, 002	0
South Sudan	211	00	-
Spain	34	00	-
Sri Lanka	94	00	0
Sudan	249	00	0
Suriname	597	00	0
Swaziland	268	00	-
Sweden	46	00	0
Switzerland	41	00	0
Syria	963	00	0
Taiwan	886	002	0
Tajikistan	992	8 - wait for dial tone - 10	8
Tanzania	255	000	0
Thailand	66	001	0
Thuraya Satellite	882 16	00	-
Togo	228	00	-
Tokelau	690	00	-
Tonga	676	00	-
Trinidad and Tobago	1	011	1
Tunisia	216	00	-
Turkey	90	00	0

Country	Country Code	Exit Code	Trunk Prefix
Turkmenistan	993	8 - wait for dial tone - 10	8
Turks and Caicos Islands	1	0	1
Tuvalu	688	00	-
Uganda	256	000	0
Ukraine	380	00	0
United Arab Emirates	971	00	0
United Kingdom	44	00	0
United States of America	1	011	1
U.S. Virgin Islands	1	011	1
Uruguay	598	00	0
Uzbekistan	998	00	0
Vanuatu	678	00	-
Vatican City	379, 39	00	-
Venezuela	58	00	0
Vietnam	84	00	0
Wallis and Futuna	681	00	-
Yemen	967	00	0
Zambia	260	00	0
Zimbabwe	263	00	0

How To Use An Image As A Link Using HTML

You can also use an image as a link by using the HTML `<a>` element and its `href` attribute along with the `<img>` element and its `src` and `alt` attributes.

In order to create our image link just simply wrap the `<a>` element around the `<img>` element as seen in the example below.

```
<a href="https://www.ebooklingo.com/">
  <img src="./images/logo.png" alt="eBookLingo.com logo">
</a>
```

Example 137

Example as seen in FireFox 80.0.1 (64-bit) browser.

How To Link To A JavaScript Using HTML

You can also call a JavaScript method using the `javascript:` protocol and the HTML `<a>` element and its `href` attribute. Just simply place the `javascript:` protocol and the JavaScript method inside the `href` attribute as seen in the example below.

```
<a href="javascript:alert('I\'m Pickle Riiiiiiiiiiiiiiiiiiiiick!');">Show Message</a>
```

Example 138

Example as seen in FireFox 80.0.1 (64-bit) browser.

Show Message

How To Link To A CSS External Style Sheet Using HTML

HTML allows you to link to an external document or resource using the HTML `<link>` element and its `href` and `rel` attributes. The `<link>` element is used to link to an external document or resource but its mostly used to link to a CSS external style sheet, so we will link to a CSS external style sheet in this example. The `href` attribute will be the URL location of the CSS external style sheet.

Now the required `rel` attribute will define the relationship between the HTML web page and the linked document. We will need to use the `stylesheet` value for the `rel` attribute which states the linked document is a CSS style sheet.

To link to an external stylesheet, you will need to place the `<link>` element inside the `<head>` element.

First here is what's in the CSS external style sheet below and remember to save the CSS external style sheet with a `.css` extension.

```
h1 {
  color: #f4500a;
}


p {
  text-align: center;
  color: #2a3f54;
}
```

Example 139

Below is an example of the `<link>` element and its `href` and `rel` attributes to link to your CSS external style sheet.

```
<!DOCTYPE html>
<html lang="en">
<head>
  <title>Simply HTML5</title>
  <link href="../../css/styles.css" rel="stylesheet">
</head>
<body>
  <h1>Linked Style Sheet</h1>
  <p>Hello World!</p>
</body>
</html>
```

Example 140

Example as seen in FireFox 80.0.1 (64-bit) browser.

Linked Style Sheet

Hello World!

How To Define A Section Of Navigational Links Using HTML

HTML allows you to define a section of navigational links using the HTML `<nav>` element which defines a section of navigational links, like for example, a table of contents, a menu, a list of categories, and so on. The `<nav>` element is intended for a major block of navigational links.

Below is an example of the `<nav>` element defining a section of navigational links.

```
<nav>
 <a href="https://www.ebooklingo.com/">Home</a> |
 <a href="https://www.ebooklingo.com/promote-your-book.php">Promote Your Book</a> |
 <a href="https://www.ebooklingo.com/sell-your-ebook.php">Sell Your Ebook</a>
</nav>
```

Example 141

Example as seen in FireFox 80.0.1 (64-bit) browser.

Home | Promote Your Book | Sell Your Ebook

HTML Lists

In this section, you will learn how to create lists of all kinds from numbered lists to bullet lists as well as description lists and much more all by using HTML.

How To Add An Unordered List To Your Web Page Using HTML

Now HTML allows you to add unordered lists to you web page by using the `<ul>` element which stands for unordered list and creates the unordered list. We will also need the `<li>` element which stands for list, and is used to represent an item in the unordered list, you can place text, images, links, and so on inside the `<li>` element. Unordered lists are the most widely used lists on the Web. Unordered lists are designed to be used for listing any collection of items that have no particular order to be listed in.

The `<ul>` element tells the browser that its following content is an unordered list and that each list item should have a leading bullet character. You will also need to wrap the `<ul>` element around the `<li>` elements.

The unordered list items are contained by the `<li>` element, each display a bullet character by default. You can however choose different bullets or you can create your own using CSS. Lists are automatically indented from the left margin, which is typically about 40 pixels, but each web browser displays them differently.

Below is an example of the `<ul>` and `<li>` elements to create an unordered list.

```
<ul>
 <li>Rick Sanchez</li>
 <li>Morty Smith</li>
 <li>Beth Smith</li>
</ul>
```

Example 142

Example as seen in FireFox 80.0.1 (64-bit) browser.

- Rick Sanchez

- Morty Smith

- Beth Smith

How To Add An Ordered List To Your Web Page Using HTML

Now HTML allows you to add ordered lists to your web page which is just like an unordered list except that the list items are numbered. We will be using the HTML `<ol>` element which stands for ordered list and creates the ordered list. We will still need the `<li>` element which stands for list and is used to represent an item in the ordered list, you can place text, images, links, and so on inside the `<li>` element. Ordered lists are best used for displaying step-by-step instructions, or anything you want to be listed in a specific order.

The `<ol>` element tells the browser that its following contents is an ordered list and that each list item will be numbered rather than bulleted. You will also need to wrap the `<ol>` element around the `<li>` elements.

The ordered list items are contained by the `<li>` element, each `<li>` element will display an Arabic numeral starting at `1` by default and will increase in value by 1. You can however choose a different number to start at, like for example, the number `4` by placing the `start` attribute in the `<ol>` element which I will show you how to do later on in this tutorial.

Ordered lists are automatically indented from the left margin, which is typically about 40 pixels, but each web browser displays them differently.

Below is an example of the `<ol>` and `<li>` elements to create an ordered list.

```
<ol>
  <li>January</li>
  <li>February</li>
  <li>March</li>
</ol>
```

Example 143

Example as seen in FireFox 80.0.1 (64-bit) browser.

1. January

2. February

3. March

Choose A Different Number To Start At For The First List Item In An Ordered List

Now let me show you the start attribute for the <ol> element which lets you pick a different number to start at, like the number 7 as in our following example.

You can also use the <li> elements value attribute when the <li> element is nested inside the <ol> element. The value attribute is used to change the number of any given list item when used with the <li> element. The following <li> elements are also renumbered accordingly when the value attribute is used. The value attribute will override the start attribute when used.

Both the start and value attributes values must be a number.

Below is an example of the start and value attributes to change the numbering in the ordered list.

```
<ol start="7">
  <li>July</li>
  <li>August</li>
  <li>September</li>
  <li value="1">January</li>
  <li>February</li>
  <li>March</li>
</ol>
```

Example 144

Example as seen in FireFox 80.0.1 (64-bit) browser.

7. July

8. August

9. September

1. January

2. February

3. March

Reverse The Numbering In An Ordered List

HTML also allows you to reverse the list items numbering order to descending instead of ascending by using the <ol> elements reversed attribute which will specify that the list items should be numbered from high to low. The reversed attribute is also a boolean attribute.

Below is an example of the `<ol>` elements `reversed` attribute to reverse the list items numbering order to descending instead of ascending.

```
<ol reversed>
  <li>March</li>
  <li>February</li>
  <li>January</li>
</ol>
```

Example 145

Example as seen in FireFox 80.0.1 (64-bit) browser.

3. March

2. February

1. January

How To Add A Description List To Your Web Page Using HTML

You can also add a description list formerly known as a definition list which is great for representing a glossary, a list of terms, descriptions, or anything else you see fit, all this can be done by using the HTML `<dl>`, `<dt>` and `<dd>` elements.

The `<dl>` element will define a description list which will also contain both the `<dt>` and `<dd>` elements. The `<dt>` element will define a term or word in a description or definition list. Following the `<dt>` element is usually the `<dd>` element which will describe the term or word in a description or definition list, you may add images, links, lists and more inside the `<dd>` element.

Their can be many `<dt>` elements associated with a single `<dd>` element. Their can also be many `<dd>` elements associated with a single `<dt>` element as well.

A little fact that you should know is that browsers will typically indent descriptions or definitions on a new line below the definition term or word.

Below is an example of the `<dl>`, `<dt>` and `<dd>` elements to create a description list.

```
<dl>
<dt>HTML</dt>
<dt>Hypertext Markup Language</dt>
<dd>A standard markup language used to create the web pages that appear on the World Wide Web.</dd>

<dt>JavaScript</dt>
<dd>A programming language used to create interactive effects within web pages.</dd>
</dl>
```

Example 146

Example as seen in FireFox 80.0.1 (64-bit) browser.

HTML
Hypertext Markup Language
  A standard markup language used to create the web pages that appear on the World Wide Web.
JavaScript
  A programming language used to create interactive effects within web pages.

How To Nest Your Lists

When nesting your lists you may nest one type of list inside another, for example, the `<dl>`, `<ul>`, and `<ol>` elements may all be nested together or you can nest your lists in the same type of list, for example, you can nest an unordered list inside another unordered list, its all up to you. When nesting lists, each individual list is indented to the right side of your browser, so be careful when nesting lists.

By default, when nesting unordered lists the first list will have solid round bullets, the next list will have empty round bullets and the rest of the lists will have square bullets.

By default, when nesting ordered lists the browser will always display the first list or any other nested ordered list regardless of their nesting position in Arabic numbers, for example, (1, 2, 3).

I will use the `<ul>` element to show you how to nest a list. Now the nested lists will look complicated so take your time and look at the structure of the list. Also, it's important to remember that each new list must start before you close the `<li>` element. So, remember to close each element when finished nesting your lists, good luck.

Below is an example on how to code a simple nested list.

```
<ul>
 <li>First Nested List</li>
 <li>First Nested List</li>
 <li>First Nested List
  <ul>
   <li>Second Nested List</li>
   <li>Second Nested List</li>
   <li>Second Nested List</li>
  </ul>
 </li>
 <li>First Nested List</li>
 <li>First Nested List</li>
</ul>
```

Example 147

Example as seen in FireFox 80.0.1 (64-bit) browser.

- First Nested List
- First Nested List
- First Nested List
  - Second Nested List
  - Second Nested List
  - Second Nested List
- First Nested List
- First Nested List

Here is how to code a more complex set of nested lists in the example below.

```
<ul>
 <li>First Nested List</li>
 <li>First Nested List</li>
 <li>First Nested List
  <ul>
   <li>Second Nested List</li>
   <li>Second Nested List</li>
   <li>Second Nested List
    <ul>
     <li>Third Nested List</li>
     <li>Third Nested List</li>
     <li>Third Nested List
      <ul>
       <li>Fourth Nested List</li>
       <li>Fourth Nested List</li>
       <li>Fourth Nested List</li>
      </ul>
     </li>
     <li>Third Nested List</li>
     <li>Third Nested List</li>
    </ul>
   </li>
   <li>Second Nested List</li>
   <li>Second Nested List</li>
  </ul>
 </li>
 <li>First Nested List</li>
 <li>First Nested List</li>
</ul>
```

Example 148

Example as seen in FireFox 80.0.1 (64-bit) browser.

- First Nested List
- First Nested List
- First Nested List
  - Second Nested List
  - Second Nested List
  - Second Nested List
    - Third Nested List
    - Third Nested List
    - Third Nested List
      - Fourth Nested List
      - Fourth Nested List
      - Fourth Nested List
    - Third Nested List
    - Third Nested List
  - Second Nested List
  - Second Nested List
- First Nested List
- First Nested List

HTML Tables

In this section, you will learn how to add tabular data to your web pages like calendars, statistics, customer's details, or other types of information using HTML.

Creating A Simple HTML Table

To create a simple HTML table we will need the `<table>` , `<tr>` , and the `<td>` elements in order to create a simple HTML table that will hold tabular data, like for example, a calendar which we will use to create our simple form. Let me quickly explain the HTML elements below starting with the `<table>` element.

- The `<table>` element will define the HTML table for displaying tabular data like in a spreadsheet.

- The `<tr>` element will indicate a table row in an HTML table.

- The `<td>` element also known as a table cell or data cell will create a column inside the table row.

To create an HTML table we will need to place the `<tr>` element inside the `<table>` element which will create a table row inside the table. We will then need to place the `<td>` element inside the `<tr>` element to create a column inside the table row.

You can place as many `<tr>` elements inside the `<table>` element as you like and you can place as many `<td>` elements inside the `<tr>` element as you wish.

The `<td>` element can contain any type of content from text, images even other HTML tables, and so on. Also, the `<td>` elements are sized just large enough to fit the contents it contains by default.

IMPORTANT! I'm going to use CSS to add borders to our HTML table so that you can get a better understanding of how HTML tables are displayed in your browser. By default, borders around the `<table>` element and its `<td>` elements are separated from each other.

Below is the CSS I'm going to use to add borders around the `<table>` element and its `<td>` elements.

```
table, td {
  border: 1px solid black;
}
```

Below is an example of the `<table>`, `<tr>` and the `<td>` elements to create a simple HTML table, which in our case is a calendar.

```
<table>
 <tr>
  <td>January</td>
  <td>February</td>
  <td>March</td>
 </tr>
 <tr>
  <td>April</td>
  <td>May</td>
  <td>June</td>
 </tr>
 <tr>
  <td>July</td>
  <td>August</td>
  <td>September</td>
 </tr>
 <tr>
  <td>October</td>
  <td>November</td>
  <td>December</td>
 </tr>
</table>
```

Example 149

Example as seen in FireFox 80.0.1 (64-bit) browser.

January	February	March
April	May	June
July	August	September
October	November	December

Specify The Number Of Columns Or Rows A Table Column Should Span Using HTML

HTML also allows you to indicate how many rows or columns that the `<td>` element should span within the HTML table. By using the `<td>` elements `rowspan` and `colspan` attributes.

How To Specify The Number Of Rows A Tables Column Should Span

To indicate how many rows the `<td>` element should span you will need to include the `rowspan` attribute. The `rowspan` attributes value can be any number from `0` to `65534`. If the value is `0` the row will span to the end of the section element its contained in, which can include the `<table>`, `<thead>`, `<tbody>` and `<tfoot>` elements. The default value for the `rowspan` attribute is `1`.

IMPORTANT! I'm going to use CSS to add borders to our HTML table so that you can get a better understanding of how HTML tables are displayed in your browser. By default, borders around the `<table>` element and its `<td>` elements are separated from each other.

Below is the CSS I'm going to use to add borders around the `<table>` element and its `<td>` elements.

```
table, td {
  border: 1px solid black;
}
```

Below is an example of the `<td>` element and its `rowspan` attribute with a value of `4` located in the January column which will now extend 4 rows.

```
<table>
 <tr>
  <td rowspan="4">January</td>
  <td>February</td>
  <td>March</td>
 </tr>
 <tr>
  <td>April</td>
  <td>May</td>
  <td>June</td>
 </tr>
 <tr>
  <td>July</td>
  <td>August</td>
  <td>September</td>
 </tr>
 <tr>
  <td>October</td>
  <td>November</td>
  <td>December</td>
 </tr>
</table>
```

Example 150

Example as seen in FireFox 80.0.1 (64-bit) browser.

January	February	March	
	April	May	June
	July	August	September
	October	November	December

Now in this next example instead of having a value of `4` for the `rowspan` attribute, we will use the value of `0` which should accomplish the same thing as in the previous example.

```
<table>
 <tr>
  <td rowspan="0">January</td>
  <td>February</td>
  <td>March</td>
 </tr>
 <tr>
  <td>April</td>
  <td>May</td>
  <td>June</td>
 </tr>
 <tr>
  <td>July</td>
  <td>August</td>
  <td>September</td>
 </tr>
 <tr>
  <td>October</td>
  <td>November</td>
  <td>December</td>
 </tr>
</table>
```

Example 151

Example as seen in FireFox 80.0.1 (64-bit) browser.

January	February	March
April	May	June
July	August	September
October	November	December

How To Specify The Number Of Columns A Tables Column Should Span

In order to indicate how many columns the `<td>` element should span you will need to include the `colspan` attribute. The `colspan` attributes value can be any number from `1` to `1000`. The default value for the `colspan` attribute is `1`.

IMPORTANT! I'm going to use CSS to add borders to our HTML table so that you can get a better understanding of how HTML tables are displayed in your browser. By default, borders around the `<table>` element and its `<td>` elements are separated from each other.

Below is the CSS I'm going to use to add borders around the `<table>` element and its `<td>` elements.

```
table, td {
  border: 1px solid black;
}
```

Below is an example of the `<td>` element and its `colspan` attribute with a value of `3` located in the January column which will now extend 3 columns.

```
<table>
 <tr>
  <td colspan="3">January</td>
  <td>February</td>
  <td>March</td>
 </tr>
 <tr>
  <td>April</td>
  <td>May</td>
  <td>June</td>
 </tr>
 <tr>
  <td>July</td>
  <td>August</td>
  <td>September</td>
 </tr>
 <tr>
  <td>October</td>
  <td>November</td>
  <td>December</td>
 </tr>
</table>
```

Example 152

Example as seen in FireFox 80.0.1 (64-bit) browser.

January			February	March
April	May	June		
July	August	September		
October	November	December		

Add A Header To Your HTML Table

You can also give a group of the table's columns a header by using the `<th>` element also known as a header cell which will create a header column inside the table row that will represent a group of table columns. The text inside the `<th>` element will be bold and centered by default.

You will also need to place the `<th>` element inside the `<tr>` element to create a header column inside the table row. You can also place as many `<th>` elements inside the `<tr>` element as you wish.

IMPORTANT! I'm going to use CSS to add borders to our HTML table so that you can get a better understanding of how HTML tables are displayed in your browser. By default, borders around the `<table>` element and its `<td>` and `<th>` elements are separated from each other.

Below is the CSS I'm going to use to add borders around the `<table>` , `<td>` and `<th>` elements.

```
table, td, th {
  border: 1px solid black;
}
```

Below is an example of the `<th>` element along with its `colspan` attribute with a value of `3` to create a header that will display the year `2022` for our calendar which will represent all three of the table's columns.

```
<table>
 <tr>
  <th colspan="3">2022</th>
 </tr>
 <tr>
  <td>January</td>
  <td>February</td>
  <td>March</td>
 </tr>
 <tr>
  <td>April</td>
  <td>May</td>
  <td>June</td>
 </tr>
 <tr>
  <td>July</td>
  <td>August</td>
  <td>September</td>
 </tr>
 <tr>
  <td>October</td>
  <td>November</td>
  <td>December</td>
 </tr>
</table>
```

Example 153

Example as seen in FireFox 80.0.1 (64-bit) browser.

2022		
January	February	March
April	May	June
July	August	September
October	November	December

Add A Caption To Your HTML Table

You can also add captions to your HTML tables by using the `<caption>` element which defines a caption or a title for the table. The `<caption>` element is placed immediately after the opening `<table>` tag also known as a start tag. By default, the `<caption>` elements content will appear centered at the top of the table.

IMPORTANT! I'm going to use CSS to add borders to our HTML table so that you can get a better understanding of how HTML tables are displayed in your browser. By default, borders around the `<table>` element and its `<td>` and `<th>` elements are separated from each other.

Below is the CSS I'm going to use to add borders around the `<table>`, `<td>`, `<th>` and `<caption>` elements.

```
table, td, th, caption {
  border: 1px solid black;
}
```

Below is an example of the `<caption>` element that will create a caption for our calendar that will display that the table is "The 2022 Calendar".

```
<table>
<caption>The 2022 Calendar</caption>
<tr>
<th colspan="3">2022</th>
</tr>
<tr>
<td>January</td>
<td>February</td>
<td>March</td>
</tr>
<tr>
<td>April</td>
<td>May</td>
<td>June</td>
</tr>
<tr>
<td>July</td>
<td>August</td>
<td>September</td>
</tr>
<tr>
<td>October</td>
<td>November</td>
<td>December</td>
</tr>
</table>
```

Example 154

Example as seen in FireFox 80.0.1 (64-bit) browser.

The 2022 Calendar		
2022		
January	February	March
April	May	June
July	August	September
October	November	December

How To Add Structure To Your HTML Table

You can also add structure to your HTML tables by adding the following `<thead>`, `<tbody>` and `<tfoot>` elements.

- The `<thead>` element will group a set of table rows that contain the `<th>` elements for the HTML table.
- The `<tbody>` element is used to group a set of table rows that make up the main content of the HTML table.
- The `<tfoot>` element is used to group a set of table rows that will summarize the columns of the HTML table.

The `<thead>`, `<tfoot>`, and `<tbody>` elements each contain a row group. And each row group must contain at least one row, defined by the `<tr>` element.

IMPORTANT! I'm going to use CSS to add borders to our HTML table so that you can get a better understanding of how HTML tables are displayed in your browser. By default, borders around the `<table>` element and its `<td>` and `<th>` elements are separated from each other.

Below is the CSS I'm going to use to add borders around the `<table>`, `<td>`, `<th>` and `<caption>` elements.

```
table, td, th, caption {
  border: 1px solid black;
}
```

Below is an example of the `<thead>`, `<tbody>` and `<tfoot>` elements to add structure to our table.

```
<table>
<caption>The 2022 Calendar</caption>
<thead>
 <tr>
  <th colspan="3">2022</th>
 </tr>
</thead>
<tbody>
 <tr>
  <td>January</td>
  <td>February</td>
  <td>March</td>
 </tr>
 <tr>
  <td>April</td>
  <td>May</td>
  <td>June</td>
 </tr>
 <tr>
  <td>July</td>
  <td>August</td>
  <td>September</td>
 </tr>
 <tr>
  <td>October</td>
  <td>November</td>
  <td>December</td>
 </tr>
</tbody>
<tfoot>
 <tr>
  <td colspan="3">This calendar only names months and no days.</td>
 </tr>
</tfoot>
</table>
```

Example 155

Example as seen in FireFox 80.0.1 (64-bit) browser.

The 2022 Calendar		
2022		
January	February	March
April	May	June
July	August	September
October	November	December
This calendar only names months and no days.		

Here is another example below of the `<thead>` , `<tbody>` and `<tfoot>` elements to add structure to our table.

```
<table>
 <thead>
  <tr>
   <th>Console</th>
   <th>Price</th>
  </tr>
 </thead>
 <tbody>
  <tr>
   <td>PlayStation 5</td>
   <td>$600.00</td>
  </tr>
  <tr>
   <td>Xbox Series X</td>
   <td>$499.00</td>
  </tr>
 </tbody>
 <tfoot>
  <tr>
   <th>Total</th>
   <td>$1099.99</td>
  </tr>
 </tfoot>
</table>
```

Example 156

Example as seen in FireFox 80.0.1 (64-bit) browser.

Console	Price
PlayStation 5	$600.00
Xbox Series X	$499.00
Total	$1099.99

How To Define & Control Your Tables Columns

HTML also allows you to define each column in your HTML tables by simply including the `<colgroup>` and `<col>` elements.

The `<colgroup>` element is used to define a group of one or more columns in a table by adding CSS styles. The `<colgroup>` element must be placed after the `<caption>` element but before the `<thead>` element or `<tr>` element.

The `<col>` element defines a column within a table and is used for adding CSS styles to the column. You will also need to place the `<col>` element inside the `<colgroup>` element to add style to a column.

Only a few CSS properties will affect the tables columns.

IMPORTANT! I'm going to use CSS to add borders to our HTML table so that you can get a better understanding of how HTML tables are displayed in your browser. By default, borders around the `<table>` element and its `<td>` and `<th>` elements are separated from each other.

Below is the CSS I'm going to use to add borders around the `<table>` , `<td>` , `<th>` and `<caption>` elements.

```
table, td, th, caption {
  border: 1px solid black;
}
```

Below is an example of the `<colgroup>` and `<col>` elements to define the columns to our table.

```
<table>
  <caption>The 2022 Calendar</caption>
  <colgroup>
    <col style="background-color: #c6c2c2; width: 200px;">
    <col style="background-color: #d4bdc5; width: 200px;">
    <col style="background-color: #bdd1d4; width: 150px;">
  </colgroup>
  <thead>
    <tr>
      <th colspan="3">2022</th>
    </tr>
  </thead>
  <tbody>
    <tr>
      <td>January</td>
      <td>February</td>
      <td>March</td>
    </tr>
    <tr>
      <td>April</td>
      <td>May</td>
      <td>June</td>
    </tr>
    <tr>
      <td>July</td>
      <td>August</td>
      <td>September</td>
    </tr>
    <tr>
      <td>October</td>
      <td>November</td>
      <td>December</td>
    </tr>
  </tbody>
  <tfoot>
    <tr>
      <td colspan="3">This calendar only names months and no days.</td>
    </tr>
  </tfoot>
</table>
```

Example 157

Example as seen in FireFox 80.0.1 (64-bit) browser.

The 2022 Calendar		
2022		
January	February	March
April	May	June
July	August	September
October	November	December
This calendar only names months and no days.		

You can also define the number of columns a column group can span using the `<col>` and `<colgroup>` elements `span` attribute. The `span` attributes value must be a number, its default value is `1`.

When adding the `span` attribute to the `<colgroup>` element the attribute's value must be the exact number of columns the table holds.

First, let me show you how to add the `span` attribute to the `<colgroup>` element in the example below.

```
<table>
<caption>The 2022 Calendar</caption>
<colgroup span="3" style="background-color: #bdd1d4; width: 200px;"></colgroup>
<thead>
  <tr>
   <th colspan="3">2022</th>
  </tr>
</thead>
<tbody>
  <tr>
   <td>January</td>
   <td>February</td>
   <td>March</td>
  </tr>
  <tr>
   <td>April</td>
   <td>May</td>
   <td>June</td>
  </tr>
  <tr>
   <td>July</td>
   <td>August</td>
   <td>September</td>
  </tr>
  <tr>
   <td>October</td>
   <td>November</td>
   <td>December</td>
  </tr>
</tbody>
<tfoot>
  <tr>
   <td colspan="3">This calendar only names months and no days.</td>
  </tr>
</tfoot>
</table>
```

Example 158

Example as seen in FireFox 80.0.1 (64-bit) browser.

The 2022 Calendar		
2022		
January	February	March
April	May	June
July	August	September
October	November	December
This calendar only names months and no days.		

Now let me show you how to add the `span` attribute to the `<col>` element in the example below.

```
<table>
 <caption>The 2022 Calendar</caption>
 <colgroup>
  <col span="1" style="background-color: #d4bdc5; width: 200px;">
  <col span="2" style="background-color: #bdd1d4; width: 150px;">
 </colgroup>
 <thead>
  <tr>
   <th colspan="3">2022</th>
  </tr>
 </thead>
 <tbody>
  <tr>
   <td>January</td>
   <td>February</td>
   <td>March</td>
  </tr>
  <tr>
   <td>April</td>
   <td>May</td>
   <td>June</td>
  </tr>
  <tr>
   <td>July</td>
   <td>August</td>
   <td>September</td>
  </tr>
  <tr>
   <td>October</td>
   <td>November</td>
   <td>December</td>
  </tr>
 </tbody>
 <tfoot>
  <tr>
   <td colspan="3">This calendar only names months and no days.</td>
  </tr>
 </tfoot>
</table>
```

Example 159

Example as seen in FireFox 80.0.1 (64-bit) browser.

The 2022 Calendar		
2022		
January	February	March
April	May	June
July	August	September
October	November	December
This calendar only names months and no days.		

HTML Semantics

In this section, you will learn how to give meaning to your web page that both the browser and the developer can understand all by using semantic HTML elements.

How To Group Content When There Are No Other Semantic Elements To Use

When there are no other semantic elements to use, you will then need to use the HTML `<div>` element which is used to define and to group content that can also be styled using CSS.

Below is an example on how to use the `<div>` element.

```
<article>
 <h1>August</h1>
 <div>
  <p>August's flower is the gladiolus or poppy, and its birthstone is the peridot, sardonyx, or sapphire.</p>
  <p>Zodiac signs in August include Leo (July 23 – August 22) and Virgo (August 23 – September 22).</p>
 </div>
</article>
```

Example 160

Example as seen in FireFox 80.0.1 (64-bit) browser.

August

August's flower is the gladiolus or poppy, and its birthstone is the peridot, sardonyx, or sapphire.

Zodiac signs in August include Leo (July 23 - August 22) and Virgo (August 23 - September 22).

How To Group Inline Content When There Are No Other Semantic Elements To Use

Just like the `<div>` element which groups blocks of content when there are no other semantic elements to use, the `<span>` element groups inline content within the blocks of content when there are no other semantic elements to use. The `<span>` element can also be styled using CSS.

Below is an example on how to use the `<span>` element which will turn the text it contains blue by using CSS.

```
<p>The zodiac earth signs include:</p>
<ul>
 <li><span class="sign">Taurus</span></li>
 <li><span class="sign">Virgo</span></li>
 <li><span class="sign">Capricorn</span></li>
</ul>
```

Example 161

Example as seen in FireFox 80.0.1 (64-bit) browser.

The zodiac earth signs include:

- Taurus
- Virgo
- Capricorn

How To Define An Independent Part Of A Web Page

HTML also allows you to define independent sections of a web page that can be reused in other places independently from the web page, for example, posts, articles, comments, or any other independent content all by using the `<article>` element.

Each `<article>` element must contain at least one of the following heading elements `<h1>`, `<h2>`, `<h3>`, `<h4>`, `<h5>` or `<h6>`.

Below is an example on how to use the `<article>` element.

```
<article>
 <h2>August</h2>
 <p>August's flower is the gladiolus or poppy, and its birthstone is the peridot, sardonyx, or sapphire.</p>
</article>
```

Example 162

Example as seen in FireFox 80.0.1 (64-bit) browser.

August

August's flower is the gladiolus or poppy, and its birthstone is the peridot, sardonyx, or sapphire.

How To Nest The <article> Element

You can also nest the `<article>` element, for example, questions with comments and so on.

Below is an example on how to nest the `<article>` element.

```
<article>
 <h1>Question</h1>
 <p>The questions answer.</p>

 <h2>Comments</h2>
 <article>
  <h3>Posted by: Rick Sanchez</h3>
  <p>I'm Pickle Riiiiiiiiiiiiiiiiiiiiick!</p>
 </article>

 <article>
  <h3>Posted by: Mr. Meeseeks</h3>
  <p>I'm Mr. Meeseeks! Look at me!</p>
 </article>
</article>
```

Example 163

Example as seen in FireFox 80.0.1 (64-bit) browser.

Question

The questions answer.

Comments

Posted by: Rick Sanchez

I'm Pickle Riiiiiiiiiiiiiiiiiiiiick!

Posted by: Mr. Meeseeks

I'm Mr. Meeseeks! Look at me!

How To Add A Header To Your Introductory Content

You can even add a header to a section of a web page by including the `<header>` element which is used to define a group of introductory or navigational aids. You can also have multiple `<header>` elements in a web page.

Below is an example on how to use the `<header>` element.

```
<header>
 <h1>eBooKlingo</h1>
 <nav>
  <a href="https://www.ebooklingo.com/">Home</a> |
  <a href="https://www.ebooklingo.com/promote-your-book.php">Promote Your Book</a> |
  <a href="https://www.ebooklingo.com/sell-your-ebook.php">Sell Your Ebook</a>
 </nav>
</header>
```

Example 164

Example as seen in FireFox 80.0.1 (64-bit) browser.

eBooKlingo

Home | Promote Your Book | Sell Your Ebook

How To Add A Footer To Your Web Page Or A Section Of Your Web Page

HTML allows you to add a footer to your web page or a section of your web page by including the `<footer>` element. The `<footer>` element is usually used for copyright information, contact information, links like social media, and so on. You can also have multiple `<footer>` elements in a web page.

Below is an example on how to use the `<footer>` element.

```
<footer>
 <p>Copyright © 2020 eBookLingo.com.</p>
</footer>
```

Example 165

Example as seen in FireFox 80.0.1 (64-bit) browser.

Copyright © 2020 eBookLingo.com.

How To Define The Main Content On Your Web Page

In HTML you can also define the main content of your web page by using the `<main>` element. There can only be one `<main>` element in a web page.

Below is an example on how to use the `<main>` element.

```html
<!DOCTYPE html>
<html lang="en">
<head>
 <title>Simply HTML5</title>
</head>
<body>
 <header>
  <h1>eBooKlingo</h1>
  <nav>
   <a href="https://www.ebooklingo.com/">Home</a> |
   <a href="https://www.ebooklingo.com/promote-your-book.php">Promote Your Book</a> |
   <a href="https://www.ebooklingo.com/sell-your-ebook.php">Sell Your Ebook</a>
  </nav>
 </header>
 <main>
  <article>
   <h2>July</h2>
   <p>July's flower is the Larkspur or the Water Lily, and its birthstone is the ruby.</p>
  </article>

  <article>
   <h2>August</h2>
   <p>August's flower is the gladiolus or poppy, and its birthstone is the peridot, sardonyx, or sapphire.</p>
  </article>

  <article>
   <h2>September</h2>
   <p>September's flower is the aster or morning glory, and its birthstone is the sapphire.</p>
  </article>
 </main>
</body>
</html>
```

Example 166

eBooKlingo

<u>Home</u> | <u>Promote Your Book</u> | <u>Sell Your Ebook</u>

July

July's flower is the Larkspur or the Water Lily, and its birthstone is the ruby.

August

August's flower is the gladiolus or poppy, and its birthstone is the peridot, sardonyx, or sapphire.

September

September's flower is the aster or morning glory, and its birthstone is the sapphire.

How To Define A Section Of Your Web Page

In HTML you can also define a section of your web page, for example, a contact us section, about us section, and so on all by using the `<section>` element.

Just like the `<article>` element each `<section>` element must contain at least one of the following heading elements `<h1>`, `<h2>`, `<h3>`, `<h4>`, `<h5>` or `<h6>`.

Below is an example on how to use the `<section>` element.

```
<article>
 <h1>Facts About Months</h1>
 <section>
  <h2>July</h2>
  <p>July's flower is the Larkspur or the Water Lily, and its birthstone is the ruby.</p>
 </section>

 <section>
  <h2>August</h2>
  <p>August's flower is the gladiolus or poppy, and its birthstone is the peridot, sardonyx, or sapphire.</p>
 </section>

 <section>
  <h2>September</h2>
  <p>September's flower is the aster or morning glory, and its birthstone is the sapphire.</p>
 </section>
</article>
```

Example 167

Example as seen in FireFox 80.0.1 (64-bit) browser.

Facts About Months

July
July's flower is the Larkspur or the Water Lily, and its birthstone is the ruby.

August
August's flower is the gladiolus or poppy, and its birthstone is the peridot, sardonyx, or sapphire.

September
September's flower is the aster or morning glory, and its birthstone is the sapphire.

How To Add Content That Is Somewhat Related To The Main Content

To add somewhat related content to the main content of your web page all you need to do is add the `<aside>` element. The `<aside>` element is usually used as a sidebar for a web page that usually holds advertising, a blogroll, or other somewhat related content to the web page.

When the `<aside>` element is placed inside the `<article>` element the contents should be specifically related to that article, for example, like comments, pull quotes, other links to web pages providing further information, and so on.

Below is an example on how to use the `<aside>` element.

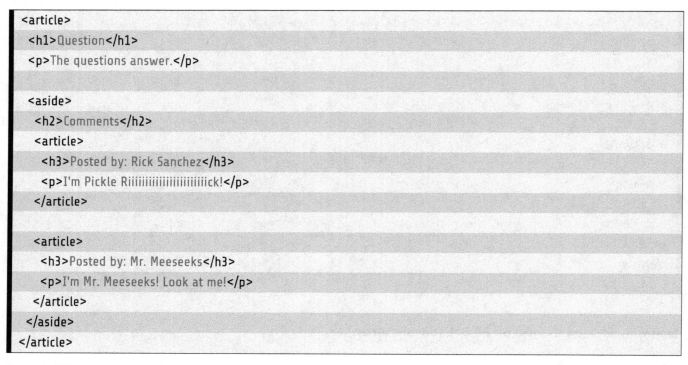

```
<article>
  <h1>Question</h1>
  <p>The questions answer.</p>

  <aside>
    <h2>Comments</h2>
    <article>
      <h3>Posted by: Rick Sanchez</h3>
      <p>I'm Pickle Riiiiiiiiiiiiiiiiiiiiiiiick!</p>
    </article>

    <article>
      <h3>Posted by: Mr. Meeseeks</h3>
      <p>I'm Mr. Meeseeks! Look at me!</p>
    </article>
  </aside>
</article>
```

Example 168

Question

The questions answer.

Comments

Posted by: Rick Sanchez

I'm Pickle Riiiiiiiiiiiiiiiiiiiiiiick!

Posted by: Mr. Meeseeks

I'm Mr. Meeseeks! Look at me!

How To Provide Additional Details

HTML also provides you a way to display additional details that the user can open and close on demand all by using the HTML `<details>` element which generates a header label that when clicked opens and closes the additional details that it contains.

You can also include the `<summary>` element which gives a heading to the `<details>` element. The `<summary>` element must be placed inside the `<details>` element. If no `<summary>` element is present the web browser will provide its own header for the `<details>` element by usually displaying the word "Details".

The `<summary>` element should be the first element placed immediately after the `<details>` start tag.

By default, the additional details contained by the `<details>` element is closed until the header label is clicked by the user to expand or in others open.

All types of content can be placed inside the `<details>` element.

Below are two examples on how to use the `<details>` and `<summary>` elements, one `<details>` element will have the `<summary>` element and one without.

```
<details>
 <h1>August</h1>
 <p>August's flower is the gladiolus or poppy, and its birthstone is the peridot, sardonyx, or sapphire.</p>
</details>

<details>
 <summary>August</summary>
 <p>August's flower is the gladiolus or poppy, and its birthstone is the peridot, sardonyx, or sapphire.</p>
</details>
```

Example 169

Example as seen in FireFox 80.0.1 (64-bit) browser.

▶ Details
▶ August

How To Add A Dialog Box To Your Web Page

In order to add a dialog box or lightbox to your web page simply add the `<dialog>` element. And to display the dialog box to a user simply add the `open` attribute to the `<dialog>` element which indicates that the `<dialog>` element is active and that the user can interact with it.

Below is an example on how to use the `<dialog>` element along with its `open` attribute.

```
<dialog open>This dialog box is open</dialog>
```

Example 170

Example as seen in FireFox 80.0.1 (64-bit) browser.

This dialog box is open

How To Add Machine-Readable Content

HTML also allows you to provide a machine-readable translated version of your content by using the `<data>` element defines a human-readable value for rendering in a web browser. You will also need to include the `<data>` elements `value` attribute which provides a machine-readable value for data processors.

Also, if the content is time or date related, use the `<time>` element instead.

Below is an example on how to use the `<data>` element along with its `value` attribute.

```
<ul>
 <li><data value="60-70">Rick Sanchez</data></li>
 <li><data value="14">Morty Smith</data></li>
</ul>
```

Example 171

Example as seen in FireFox 80.0.1 (64-bit) browser.

- Rick Sanchez
- Morty Smith

CSS Basics

In this section you will learn the very basics of CSS to get you started in creating your very own Cascading Style Sheets the correct way, today.

How To Include CSS To Your HTML Web Pages

CSS can either be included as a separate file or embedded in the HTML web page itself. There are three different methods of adding CSS to your HTML web pages:

- **Inline styles** - Use the `style` attribute which is added to the given elements start tag.

- **Embedded styles** - Use the `<style>` element which is placed within the `<head>` element of a web page.

- **External style sheets** - Use the `<link>` element which points to an external CSS file.

1. **Inline styles** - have the highest priority which means that the styles will override all other styles using the embedded and external methods.

2. **Embedded styles** - have the second highest priority which means that the styles will override the external method but not the inline method.

3. **External style sheets** - have the lowest priority which means that the inline and embedded methods will override the external styles.

Inline Styles

When adding inline styles we will need to use the `style` attribute which specifies an inline CSS style for an HTML element. The `style` attributes value can have one or more CSS declarations each separated by a semicolon `;` and each declaration is made up of a property and value separated by a colon `:`.

Now you can place the `style` attribute in almost any HTML element except for the `<param>` element and the HTML elements outside the `<body>` element like the `<title>`, `<base>`, `<head>`, `<html>`, `<script>`, `<style>` and `<meta>` elements. Also, inline styles are known as local styles, which will override any style sheet that applies to the same HTML element. Inline styles only apply to the HTML element that they are stated in, and will not affect any other HTML elements what so ever.

Below in the example the first `<p>` element will have the `style` attribute with one CSS declaration as its value which will display the text in blue. And the second `<p>` element will have the `style` attribute with two CSS declarations as its value which will display the text in blue and centered.

```
<!DOCTYPE html>
<html lang="en">
<head>
  <title>Simply HTML5</title>
</head>
<body>
  <p style="color: blue;">This text will be displayed in blue.</p>
  <p style="color: blue; text-align: center;">This text will be centered and displayed in blue.</p>
</body>
</html>
```

Example 172

Example as seen in FireFox 80.0.1 (64-bit) browser.

This text will be displayed in blue.

This text will be centered and displayed in blue.

Embedded Style Sheets

Embedded style sheets which are also known as internal style sheets are another way of adding CSS to your web pages. In order to use embedded style sheets you will need to use the `<style>` element. The `<style>` element must be placed within the `<head>` element.

The `<style>` element allows you to insert style rules within a web page by placing the style rules within the `<style>` element.

An important thing to know is that embedded style sheets apply only to the web page that they are located in and will not affect any other web pages.

Below is an example of the `<style>` element to create our embedded style sheet.

```html
<!DOCTYPE html>
<html lang="en">
<head>
 <title>Simply HTML5</title>
 <style>
  h1 {
    color: #f4500a;
  }

  p {
    text-align: center;
    color: #2a3f54;
  }
 </style>
</head>
<body>
 <h1>Embedded Style Sheet</h1>
 <p>Hello World!</p>
</body>
</html>
```

Example 173

Example as seen in FireFox 80.0.1 (64-bit) browser.

Embedded Style Sheet

Hello World!

External Style Sheets

I explained this earlier but I will go over this again HTML allows you to link to an external document or resource using the HTML `<link>` element and its `href` and `rel` attributes. The `<link>` element is used to link to an external document or resource but its mostly used to link to a CSS external style sheet, so we will link to a CSS external style sheet in this example. The `href` attribute will be the URL location of the CSS external style sheet. Now the required `rel` attribute will define the relationship between the HTML web page and the linked document. We will need to use the `stylesheet` value for the `rel` attribute which states the linked document is a CSS style sheet.

To link to an external stylesheet, you will need to place the `<link>` element inside the `<head>` element.

First here is what's in the CSS external style sheet below and remember to save the CSS external style sheet with a `.css` extension.

```
h1 {
  color: #f4500a;
}


p {
  text-align: center;
  color: #2a3f54;
}
```

Example 174

Below is an example of the `<link>` element and its `href` and `rel` attributes to link to your CSS external style sheet.

```
<!DOCTYPE html>
<html lang="en">
<head>
  <title>Simply HTML5</title>
  <link href="../../css/styles.css" rel="stylesheet">
</head>
<body>
  <h1>Linked Style Sheet</h1>
  <p>Hello World!</p>
</body>
</html>
```

Example 175

Example as seen in FireFox 80.0.1 (64-bit) browser.

Linked Style Sheet

Hello World!

Importing External Style Sheets

Instead of adding external style sheets with the `<link>` element, you can add external style sheets using the `@import` rule also known as `@import` directive or the `@import` at rule. The `@import` rule basically imports one style sheet into another.

The `@import` rule can be placed in external style sheets, as long as the `@import` rules are at the top of the style sheet before any style rules except the `@charset` rule, if present.

You can also place the `@import` rules between the `<style>` element like an internal style sheet, except the `@import` rule must come before any style rules except the `@charset` rule, if present as in the example below or otherwise it won't work at all.

Below is an example on how to place the `@import` rule between the `<style>` element.

```html
<!DOCTYPE html>
<html lang="en">
<head>
 <title>Simply HTML5</title>
 <style>
 @import url("css/layout.css");
 @import url("css/color.css");
 h1 {
   color: #f4500a;
 }

 p {
   text-align: center;
   color: #2a3f54;
  }
 </style>
</head>
<body>
 <h1>Imported External Style Sheet</h1>
 <p>Hello World!</p>
</body>
</html>
```

Example 176

Below is an example on how to place the `@import` rule within another CSS stylesheet.

```
@import url("css/layout.css");
@import url("css/color.css");
h1 {
  color: #f4500a;
}

p {
  text-align: center;
  color: #2a3f54;
}
```

Example 177

How To Add CSS Styles To All Your HTML Elements Using The Universal Selector

Let's say you want to add the same style rule to all your HTML elements in your web page instead of grouping multiple selectors together, all you need to do is use the universal selector also known as the wildcard selector, which is just simply an asterisk `*`. For example, if you want all your HTML elements text in your web page like the `<h1>`, `<p>` and `<ul>` elements to have the color blue and be in bold, all you have to do is code in the wildcard selector.

Below is an example on how to code in the wildcard selector `*` turn all our HTML elements text blue and bold;

```
<!DOCTYPE html>
<html lang="en">
<head>
 <title>Simply HTML5</title>
 <style>
  * {
    font-weight: bold;
    color: blue;
  }
 </style>
</head>
<body>
 <h1>Embedded Style Sheet</h1>
 <p>Hello World!</p>
</body>
</html>
```

Example 178

Example as seen in FireFox 80.0.1 (64-bit) browser.

Embedded Style Sheet

Hello World!

How To Name A Group Of HTML Elements Using The Class Attribute

You're probably asking yourself why would I want to name my HTML elements. Let's say you have a web page that answers frequently asked questions from your users and you have a paragraph that holds the users question using the `<p>` element and another paragraph that holds the answer also using the `<p>` element. And you want all the questions text to be in bold and in the color of blue with a bottom margin of zero but not the answers. In order to do this, we will need to do two things, first, we will need to add the `class` attribute with the value of `question` to all our question paragraphs `<p>` start tags.

Next, we will need to create our style rule. Since we are using the `class` attribute the name of our class style rule also known as a class selector, will begin with a period `.` followed by the `class` attributes value which in our case is `question` and then followed by the declarations which in our case will be `font-weight: bold; color: blue; margin-bottom: 0;`.

I explained this earlier but I will explain it again the `class` attribute assigns a class name or a space-separated list of class names to an HTML element. Multiple HTML elements can have the same class name.

The `class` attributes value has a couple of rules listed below.

- The `class` attributes value must begin with a letter A-Z or a-z
- The `class` attributes value can then be followed by digits 0-9, letters A-Z or a-z, hyphens ("-"), and underscores ("_")

Below is an example on how to code the `class` attribute along with the styles using an embedded style sheet.

```
<!DOCTYPE html>
<html lang="en">
<head>
 <title>Simply HTML5</title>
 <style>
  .question {
    font-weight: bold;
    color: blue;
    margin-bottom: 0;
  }
 </style>
</head>
<body>
 <p class="question">Question 1</p>
 <p>Answer 1</p>

 <p class="question">Question 2</p>
 <p>Answer 2</p>

 <p class="question">Question 3</p>
 <p>Answer 3</p>
</body>
</html>
```

Example 179

Example as seen in FireFox 80.0.1 (64-bit) browser.

Question 1

Answer 1

Question 2

Answer 2

Question 3

Answer 3

How To Name An Individual HTML Element Using The Id Attribute

Unlike the `class` attribute, which allows you to add style to any number of HTML elements, which is known as a style class. You can also use the id selectors to add style to individual HTML elements by including the `id` attribute. This type of method is known as individual styles because we can only assign one unique name to an individual HTML element once per web page. You can have many id selectors per web page, but each will have to have a unique name. The `id` attributes value can't contain any space characters.

One more thing is that when we create our style rule instead of it beginning with a period we will begin it with a pound sign `#`, which I will show you how to do in our example in a second.

Now let's say we have copyright information at the bottom of each of our web pages that we want to be centered and have a text size of 13px. We can do this by first adding the `id` attribute with the value of `copy` to the copyright information's `<p>` element as in our upcoming example.

Next let's create our style rule, since we are using the `id` attribute, the name of our style rule also known as an id selector will begin with a pound sign `#` followed by the `id` attributes value followed by our declarations which in our case will be `text-align: center; font-size: 13px;`.

Below is an example on how to code the `id` attribute along with the styles using an embedded style sheet.

```
<!DOCTYPE html>
<html lang="en">
<head>
  <title>Simply HTML5</title>
  <style>
   #copy {
     text-align: center;
     font-size: 13px;
   }
  </style>
</head>
<body>
<p id="copy">Copyright © 2020 eBookLingo.com</p>
</body>
</html>
```

Example 180

Example as seen in FireFox 80.0.1 (64-bit) browser.

Copyright © 2020 eBookLingo.com

HTML Metadata

In this section, you will learn how metadata can provide information about your web page, which includes information to help search engines as well as web browsers and much more.

How To Add Metadata To Your Web Page

In order to add metadata to your web pages, you will need to include the HTML `<head>` element which will contain the metadata for the web page. Metadata is data about the web page which usually includes the web pages title, description, character set, CSS style sheets, and other types of metadata.

The following HTML elements that can be placed inside the `<head>` element include the `<title>`, `<base>`, `<link>`, `<style>`, `<meta>`, `<script>` and the `<noscript>` elements.

The `<head>` element has a required element that is placed within the `<head>` element called the `<title>` element which gives the web page a title that is displayed in the browsers title bar or in the pages tab. Only one `<title>` element is allowed per HTML document page. The `<title>` element can only contain plain text and HTML entities.

The `<title>` elements contents are displayed in search engines and also provides a title for the web page when added to favorites or bookmarked.

Below is an example on how to code the `<head>` and `<title>` elements to your web page.

```
<!DOCTYPE html>
<html lang="en">
<head>
  <title>Simply HTML5</title>
</head>
<body>
</body>
</html>
```

Example 181

Metadata Basics

The `<meta>` element also known as metadata provides additional information about your web page, for example, keywords, author information, language type, description, and much more. The `<meta>`

element is also used to embed information about your web page that most search engines use to index and categorize your web page with. The information within the `<meta>` elements may be used by servers and web browsers as well.

The `<meta>` element should be placed within the `<head>` element usually after the `<title>` element for most `<meta>` elements, in certain cases the `<meta>` element should be placed before the `<title>` element. You are allowed to have more then one `<meta>` element in your web pages.

Now let me explain the two most popular types of `<meta>` elements, which I will show you how to code into our web page for our example.

First the description `<meta>` element. The description `<meta>` element requires the `name` and `content` attributes. The `name` attribute has to have the value of `description` and the `content` attribute can have any text value that describes your web page. Search engines will display only some of the `content` attributes value if it is too long, also some search engines will ignore the description `<meta>` element. There is no standard on how long your description should be and it varies from search engine to search engine on how many characters are allowed.

Next, I will explain the keywords `<meta>` element, which also needs the `name` and `content` attributes. Now the `name` attribute has to have the value of `keywords` and the `content` attributes value can be any words or phrases that describe your web page just make sure to separate each keyword or phrase with a comma `,`. Keywords are usually used by search engines to help make your web pages more searchable.

Below is an example on how to code the keywords and description `<meta>` elements.

```
<!DOCTYPE html>
<html lang="en">
<head>
 <title>Simply HTML5</title>
 <meta name="description" content="eBookLingo.com is an online social marketplace for authors and readers.">
 <meta name="keywords" content="self publishers, promote books, sell ebooks, buy ebooks">
</head>
<body>
</body>
</html>
```

Example 182

How To Indicate The Web Pages Author

The purpose of the author `<meta>` element is to indicate who created the web page by providing one of the following formats which include the author's full name, email address, company name, or URL address in the `<meta>` element. The most common format is to provide the author's full name or company with an email address, but it's not recommended to include the email address due to spamming. The author `<meta>` element is not supported by the major search engines but it is still considered a `<meta>` element standard.

In order to create the author `<meta>` element, you will need the `<meta>` element and the `name` attribute with the value of `author` and the required `content` attribute to hold the name of the author, email address, company name, or URL address. In our example, we will use the author's full name as the `content` attributes value. The author's first name should be placed first along with the last name last and if there is a middle name it should be placed in the middle.

Below is an example on how to code the author `<meta>` element.

```
<!DOCTYPE html>
<html lang="en">
<head>
  <title>Simply HTML5</title>
   <meta name="author" content="Rick Sanchez">
</head>
<body>
</body>
</html>
```

Example 183

How To Give Your Web Page A Copyright

The copyright `<meta>` element is not the best way to copyright protect your web page. It's more of a way to state that your web page has been, trademarked, copyrighted, patented, or anything about your intellectual property.

In order to create the copyright `<meta>` element, you will have to use the `<meta>` element with the `name` attribute with the value of `copyright` . You will also need to include the required `content` attribute in which you will state the name of the copyright holder as its value.

Below is an example on how to code the copyright `<meta>` element.

```html
<!DOCTYPE html>
<html lang="en">
<head>
    <title>Simply HTML5</title>
    <meta name="copyright" content="eBookLingo.com">
</head>
<body>
</body>
</html>
```

Example 184

How To Refresh Your Web Pages

What if your web page has information that is updated every 2 minutes or so from your database or from other sources, for example, stock quotes, news, and so on, well you can refresh your web page by using the refresh `<meta>` element.

Now in order to refresh your web page, we will need to use the `<meta>` element along with the `http-equiv` attribute with the value of `refresh`, we will also need the required `content` attribute with a number value. For example, if we were to have `13` as the value for the `content` attribute it would refresh our web page every `13` seconds, so in other words, you should state the amount of time until your web page refreshes, in seconds for the `content` attributes value. One important thing to remember is that when you refresh your web page in less than 10 seconds some search engines will not index your web page.

When the `http-equiv` attribute is added to a `<meta>` element, the element is called a pragma directive.

Below is an example on how to code the refresh `<meta>` element that will refresh every 2 minutes.

```
<!DOCTYPE html>
<html lang="en">
<head>
  <title>Simply HTML5</title>
  <meta http-equiv="refresh" content="120">
</head>
<body>
</body>
</html>
```

Example 185

How To Tell Search Engines If Your Web Page Should Be Indexed Or Not

Okay, what if you don't want search engines indexing your web pages for some reason. This is why the robots `<meta>` element was created to give orders to search engine spiders also known as robots, which are automated mechanisms that spider your site to list in the search engines.

Now in order to create our robots `<meta>` element, we will need the `<meta>` element along with the `name` attribute with the value of `robots`. We will also need the required `content` attribute, which can have one of many values, I will list some of the values which include `all`, `none`, `index`, `noindex`, `noarchive`, `follow`, `nofollow`, `noimageindex`, and `noimageclick`.

- The `noarchive` value will stop search engines from showing a cached link for your web page.

- The `all` value is the robots default value, which allows all of the web site's web pages to be indexed.

- The `none` value tells the search engine spider not to index any web pages from your web site as well as not to follow any links on the web page.

- The `index` value will suggest that the web page should be indexed by search engine spiders.

- The `noindex` value will stop anything from your web page from being indexed.

- The `follow` value should tell the search engine spiders that they should follow the links from the current web page to other web pages.

- The `nofollow` value means only the current web page should be indexed and that no other links should be indexed.

- The `noimageindex` value will allow the text to be indexed on the web page but not the images.

- The `noimageclick` value will not allow any links to any images to be indexed, only links to the web page will be indexed.

You can also group the values together, for example, `index,nofollow`, and so on as long as there is a comma separating each value.

Below is an example on how to code the robots `<meta>` element.

```
<!DOCTYPE html>
<html lang="en">
<head>
  <title>Simply HTML5</title>
  <meta name="robots" content="noindex,follow">
</head>
<body>
</body>
</html>
```

Example 186

How To Tell Search Engines When To Revisit Your Web Page

You can also tell search engine spiders when to come back to your web site and re-index your web pages. In order to accomplish this, you will need to use the revisit-after `<meta>` element. One more thing you should know before I explain the revisit-after `<meta>` element is that major search engines are thought not to support the revisit-after `<meta>` element, but it never hurts to include the revisit-after `<meta>` element anyway.

To create the revisit-after `<meta>` element, you will obviously need the `<meta>` element along with the `name` attribute with the value of `revisit-after`. You will also need the required `content` attribute that will need to have a value that states how many days not months until the search engine spider should come back and re-index your web site. For example, 214 days will tell the search engine spiders to come back and re-index your site in about 7 months, which is the correct way to specify 7 months.

Below is an example on how to code the revisit-after `<meta>` element.

```
<!DOCTYPE html>
<html lang="en">
<head>
  <title>Simply HTML5</title>
  <meta name="revisit-after" content="13 days">
</head>
<body>
</body>
</html>
```

Example 187

How To State Your Web Pages Text Encoding

One thing you should know is that it is always a good idea to define your character encodings for every one of your web pages. Character encodings are the way that a languages alphabet, numbers, glyphs, and so on are translated by your computer into bits, each one of your characters will be translated into bits, this is known as character encoding.

Now there are many character encodings for each specific language that I can explain to you but that is a whole other book so we will stick with the most common and recommended encoding, which is the UTF-8 encoding, because it covers other character encodings for other languages as well, not just only English. However, this encoding has its problems as well, but for now, it is still the recommended encoding to use.

Okay, now that you have some kind of basic understanding of what character encodings are, let me explain to you how to state your web pages encoding. In order to do this, we will need to use the content-type `<meta>` element along with the `http-equiv` attribute with the value of `content-type`. We will also need the `content` attribute with the value of `text/html` for HTML and XHTML, which is known as a MIME type. But for XHTML your web pages must be processed with one of the following MIME type values, which include `application/xhtml+xml`, `application/xml`, or `text/xml` but the W3C, which sets the standards suggest that you use `application/xhtml+xml` only.

Now we will also need the `charset` attribute, which needs to be separated from the `content` attribute by a semicolon `;` also one important thing you should remember is that you should not close your `content` attributes value with the quotation mark `"` until the end of the `charset` attributes value. The `charset` attributes value can have any character encoding that is suitable for your web pages written language, but for our example, we are going to use the standard `UTF-8` encoding as our `charset` attributes value, but if you want to learn more about character encodings I suggest you pick up a book you feel comfortable with that explains UNICODE.

Another important thing you should remember is that our `charset` attribute should not have a quotation mark after the equals sign `=` .

One last important thing to remember is that you should place your content-type `<meta>` element before the `<title>` element because if not the browser itself might decide the character encoding for your web page plus your `<title>` elements text might not be displayed in the right character encoding, but this is rarely a problem if your web pages text is in English.

Also, when the `http-equiv` attribute is added to a `<meta>` element, the element is called a pragma directive. Below is an example on how to code the content-type `<meta>` element.

```
<!DOCTYPE html>
<html lang="en">
<head>
 <meta http-equiv="content-type" content="text/html; charset=utf-8">
 <title>Simply HTML5</title>
</head>
<body>
</body>
</html>
```

Example 188

Now that you learned the hard way to specify your web pages character encoding, let me now show you the simple way which just requires the `<meta>` element and its `charset` attribute and your desired character encoding for the `charset` attributes value.

```
<!DOCTYPE html>
<html lang="en">
<head>
 <meta charset="utf-8">
 <title>Simply HTML5</title>
</head>
<body>
</body>
</html>
```

Example 189

How To Define The Default URL For A Web Page

In HTML you can define the default URL for all your relative URLs in your HTML web page by using the `<base>` element and its `href` attribute. The `href` attribute specifies the URL for all the relative URLs on the web page. There can only be one `<base>` element in an HTML web page.

You can also include the `target` attribute and one of its reserved target name values.

- The `_blank` value will tell the browser to always open the link in a new browser window.

- The `_self` value is the `<base>` elements default value which will instruct the targeted link to load in the same window or tab.

- The `_parent` value will load the targeted link into the parent window or frame containing the `_parent` value. Now if the `_parent` value is indicated in a top-level frame or window it is equal to the target name value `_self`.

- The `_top` value will open in a full browser window.

All the target reserved names begin with an underscore `_` character. You should not use an underscore as the first character for any other target name values other then the four reserved target name values, if you do the value will be ignored by all browsers.

The `<base>` element must have either an `href` or a `target` attribute or both.

Below is an example on how to code the `<base>` element and its `href` and `target` attributes to your web page.

```
<!DOCTYPE html>
<html lang="en">
<head>
 <title>Simply HTML5</title>
 <base href="https://www.ebooklingo.com/" target="_blank">
</head>
<body>
 <a href="">eBookLingo.com</a> <br>
 <a href="/promote-your-book.php">Promote Your Book</a> <br>
 <a href="/sell-your-ebook.php">Sell Your Book</a> <br>
 <img src="/images/logo.png" alt="eBookLingo.com logo">
</body>
</html>
```

Example 190

Example as seen in FireFox 80.0.1 (64-bit) browser.

eBookLingo.com

Promote Your Book

Sell Your Book

HTML Scripting

In this section, you will learn how to add scripting languages to your web page like JavaScript using HTML.

How To Add JavaScript To Your Web Page Part 1

HTML gives you two ways to add JavaScript to your web pages either internally or externally. First, I will show you the internal method. For the internal method, we will need to use the `<script>` element which is used to embed a client-side script like JavaScript. The `<script>` element is also used in the external method as well, but written differently. Everything that is placed between the `<script>` element will be the JavaScript code that the browser will process. You cannot place any HTML within the `<script>` element unless its part of the JavaScript code. You may add as many `<script>` elements as you wish in-between either the `<head>` or `<body>` elements.

Now let's add some JavaScript code to our web page using the `<script>` element, which I will show you how to do in the example below. We will be adding some JavaScript code that will display the date, time, and year in a bold and italic font on our web page.

Below is an example on how to add client-side scripts using the internal method.

```
<!DOCTYPE html>
<html lang="en">
<head>
  <title>Simply HTML5</title>
  <script>
    document.write("<p> <i> <b>" + Date() + "<\/b> <\/i> <\/p>");
  </script>
</head>
<body>
</body>
</html>
```

Example 191

Example as seen in FireFox 80.0.1 (64-bit) browser.

Fri Oct 30 2020 20:47:13 GMT-0700 (Pacific Daylight Time)

How To Add JavaScript To Your Web Page Part 2

Now let me show you how to add JavaScript to your web pages using the external method, which is the most widely, used method as well as the best way to add JavaScript to your web pages.

To create an external JavaScript file, you will need to first open Notepad for the PC or TextEdit for the MAC, both of which are free, but any text editor will do free or paid. Next type in the following JavaScript code below.

```
document.write("<p> <i> <b>" + Date() + "<\/b> <\/i> <\/p>");
```

Example 192

Now you will need to save and name your JavaScript file and give it a `.js` extension, for example, `file-name.js` is the way to save your file.

Now let's link the JavaScript file to the web page, to do this we will need to use the `<script>` element along with the `src` attribute in which its value will be the location of our JavaScript file, which can be either a relative or absolute value. You can place the `<script>` element either between the `<head>` or `<body>` elements.

Below is an example on how to add client-side scripts using the external method.

```
<!DOCTYPE html>
<html lang="en">
<head>
 <title>Simply HTML5</title>
 <script src="./scripts/date.js"></script>
</head>
<body>
</body>
</html>
```

Example 193

Example as seen in FireFox 80.0.1 (64-bit) browser.

Fri Oct 30 2020 20:47:13 GMT-0700 (Pacific Daylight Time)

Provide Alternate Content To Users Whose Browers Do Not Support Client-Side Scripts

What if a user's web browser doesn't support client-side scripting or the user disabled scripts in their web browser. You can provide those users with alternate content by adding the `<noscript>` element. The content placed inside the `<noscript>` element will only be displayed to the user if the web browser doesn't support client-side scripts or if the user disabled scripts in their web browser.

Below is an example on how to add the `<noscript>` element.

```
<!DOCTYPE html>
<html lang="en">
<head>
 <title>Simply HTML5</title>
</head>
<body>
 <script>
   document.write("<p> <i> <b>" + Date() + "<\/b> <\/i> <\/p>");
 </script>
 <noscript>Sorry, your web browser does not support JavaScript!</noscript>
</body>
</html>
```

Example 194

Example as seen in FireFox 80.0.1 (64-bit) browser.

Sorry, your web browser does not support JavaScript!

HTML Embedded Content

In this section you will learn how to embedded objects to your web page, like for example, different kinds of audio and video files, PDF documents, Flash animations, images, other web pages, and much more using HTML.

How To Embed Media Files To Your Web Page Using The <object> Element

HTML provides a variety of ways to embed a media file to your HTML web pages one way to accomplish this is to use the `<object>` element which will embed a media file to the web page in our example we will be embedding a PDF file to our web page. We will also need to include the following attributes listed below.

- The `data` attribute specifies the URL of the media file that will be embedded to the web page.

- The `type` attribute which indicates the media type (formerly known as MIME type) for the media file that you indicated as the value for the `data` attribute. For example, `file.pdf` will have a media type of `application/pdf` which we will be using for our example which is the media type for a PDF file.

- The `width` attribute specifies the width of the embedded object in pixels.

- The `height` attribute specifies the height of the embedded object in pixels.

A couple of important things to remember when embedding, images, web pages, audio, and video files are listed below.

- To embed a picture or image, it is better to use the `<img>` element.

- To embed an HTML web page, it is better to use the `<iframe>` element.

- And to embed an audio or video file, it is better to use the `<audio>` or `<video>` elements.

You can also place text and other HTML elements within the `<object>` element which will be displayed if the `<object>` element or media file is not supported by the web browser.

Below is an example on how to add the `<object>` element and its `data`, `type`, `width`, and `height` attributes to embed a PDF file to our web page.

```
<object type="application/pdf" data="./media/example.pdf" width="400" height="350">
  Alternative link to: <a href="./media/example.pdf">example.pdf</a>
</object>
```

Example 195

Example as seen in FireFox 80.0.1 (64-bit) browser.

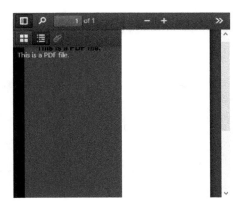

How To Embed Media Files To Your Web Page Using The `<embed>` Element

Another way to embed a media file to your HTML web pages is to use the `<embed>` element which will embed a media file to the web page in our example we will be embedding a PDF file to our web page. We will also need to include the following attributes listed below.

- The `src` attribute specifies the URL of the media file that will be embedded to the web page.

- The `type` attribute which indicates the media type (formerly known as MIME type) for the media file that you indicated as the value for the `src` attribute. For example, `file.pdf` will have a media type of `application/pdf` which we will be using for our example which is the media type for a PDF file.

- The `width` attribute specifies the width of the embedded object in pixels.

- The `height` attribute specifies the height of the embedded object in pixels.

A couple of important things to remember when embedding, images, web pages, audio, and video files are listed below.

- To embed a picture or image, it is better to use the `<img>` element.

- To embed an HTML web page, it is better to use the `<iframe>` element.

- And to embed an audio or video file, it is better to use the `<audio>` or `<video>` elements.

Below is an example on how to add the `<embed>` element and its `src`, `type`, `width`, and `height` attributes to embed a PDF file to our web page.

```
<embed type="application/pdf" src="./media/example.pdf" width="400" height="350">
```

Example 196

Example as seen in FireFox 80.0.1 (64-bit) browser.

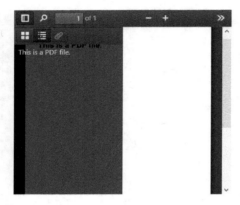

How To Pass Parameters To Embedded Media Files

Now there is a couple of ways to pass parameters to your embed media files. To pass parameters to your embedded media file that is embedded using the `<object>` element is to simply include the `<param>` element which will supply the parameter, which is information that the embedded media file will use. You will also need to include the required `name` and `value` attributes.

The `<param>` elements required `name` attribute will define the parameters name, which is information that will be used by the `<object>` elements embedded media file. The `name` attributes value can be any name supported by the embedded media file.

And the required `value` attribute will define the value of the `name` attributes parameter. The `value` attributes value can be any value supported by the embedded media file.

Since we are going to embed a PDF file to our web page for our upcoming example our `name` attribute can use any one of the following values listed below which are parameters that are commonly used to embed a PDF file to an HTML web page.

- The value of `page` for the `name` attribute will specify a number for the page in the PDF file via the `value` attributes value. The PDF file's first page has a value of `1`.

- The value of `zoom` for the `name` attribute will set the zoom and scroll factors, using percentages or number values via the `value` attributes value. For example, a value of `100` indicates a zoom value of 100%.

- The value of `view` for the `name` attribute will set the view of the displayed PDF file when the `value` attributes value is set to `Fit`.

- The value of `scrollbar` for the `name` attribute will turn the scrollbars on when the `value` attributes value is set to `1` or off when the `value` attributes value is set to `0`.

- The value of `toolbar` for the `name` attribute will turn the toolbar on when the `value` attributes value is set to `1` or off when the `value` attributes value is set to `0`.

- The value of `statusbar` for the `name` attribute will turn the status bar on when the `value` attributes value is set to `1` or off when the `value` attributes value is set to `0`.

- The value of `navpanes` for the `name` attribute will turn the navigation panes and tabs on when the `value` attributes value is set to `1` or off when the `value` attributes value is set to `0`.

Below is an example on how to add the `<param>` element and its `name` and `value` attributes to give our embedded PDF file some parameters.

```
<object type="application/pdf" data="./media/example.pdf" width="400" height="350">
  <param name="zoom" value="100">
  <param name="scrollbar" value="0">
  Alternative link to: <a href="./media/example.pdf">example.pdf</a>
</object>
```

Example 197

Example as seen in FireFox 80.0.1 (64-bit) browser.

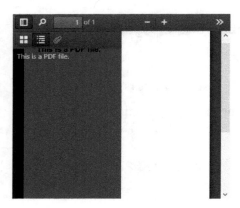

Specifying The Parameters Using The Embedded Files URL

Now if for some reason the `<param>` element does not pass the parameters to the embedded file you can always state the parameters through the embedded files URL.

Now to add a parameter to the embedded files URL address will require you to add just one pound sign `#` at the end of the embedded files URL address followed by the parameters name and then an equal sign `=` and then the value for the parameter, for example, `./media/example.pdf#zoom=100`. You will then need to add an ampersand `&` between each additional parameter, for example, `./media/example.pdf#zoom=100&scrollbar=0`.

Using this method you can add parameters to both the `<object>` and `<embed>` elements.

Below is an example on how to add parameters to your embedded files URL for the `<object>` element.

```
<object type="application/pdf" data="./media/example.pdf#zoom=100&scrollbar=0" width="400" height="350">
    Alternative link to: <a href="./media/example.pdf#zoom=100&scrollbar=0">example.pdf</a>
</object>
```

Example 198

Example as seen in FireFox 80.0.1 (64-bit) browser.

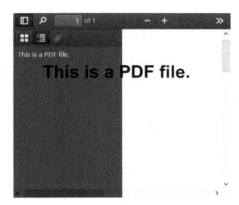

And below is an example on how to add parameters to your embedded files URL for the `<embed>` element.

```
<embed type="application/pdf" src="./media/example.pdf#zoom=100&scrollbar=0" width="400" height="350">
```
Example 199

Example as seen in FireFox 80.0.1 (64-bit) browser.

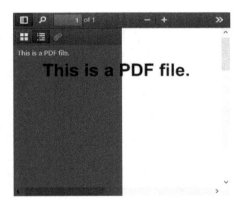

HTML Special Characters

In this section, you will learn how to add special characters and symbols that can't be typed or are not part of your web pages encoding. There is currently more than 143,000 special characters that can be displayed in decimal also known as numbered form, or they can be displayed in hexadecimal (hex) or named form.

How To Add HTML Special Characters To Your Web Page

You can display HTML special characters in either their numeric form which includes decimal and hex, which is also considered the best way to display HTML special characters or you can display HTML special characters using their named form. Both form types begin with an ampersand sign `&` and end with a semicolon `;`. For example, you can display the less than sign `<` in three different ways, either by using the decimal code form `&#60;` the hex code form `&#x3c;` or the entity named form `&lt;` not all special characters have a named form.

When adding HTML special characters and symbols to your web page it's always wise to include the web pages character set. In order for the web browser to display the HTML web page correctly. This is done by stating your web pages text encoding by including the `<meta>` element and its `charset` attribute and your desired character encoding for the `charset` attributes value. For example, the `UTF-8` character encoding covers almost all of the HTML special characters and symbols you could possibly use. Also, if the character encoding is not specified the `UTF-8` character encoding is the default character set used by HTML.

Below is an example on how to state your web pages text encoding using the `<meta>` element and its `charset` attribute and your desired character encoding for the `charset` attributes value.

```
<!DOCTYPE html>
<html lang="en">
<head>
  <meta charset="utf-8">
  <title>Simply HTML5</title>
</head>
<body>
</body>
</html>
```

Example 200

Below is a few charts of some HTML special characters, along with their decimal, hex and named forms if available.

Standard HTML Special Characters

Symbol	Description	Decimal Code	Hex Code	Special Code / Entity Name
	Horizontal Tab	&#09;	&#x9;	&Tab;
	Line Feed	&#10;	&#xa;	&NewLine;
	Carriage Return / Enter	&#13;	&#xd;	
"	Quotation mark	&#34;	&#x22;	&quot;
#	Number sign; Hash key; Pound sign	&#35;	&#x23;	
$	Dollar sign; Peso sign; String sign	&#36;	&#x24;	
%	Percent sign;	&#37;	&#x25;	
&	Ampersand; Epershand; And sign	&#38;	&#x26;	&amp;
'	Apostrophe; Prime symbol	&#39;	&#x27;	
(	Left parenthesis; Left round bracket; Left paren	&#40;	&#x28;	&lparen;
)	Right parenthesis; Right round bracket; Right paren	&#41;	&#x29;	&rparen;
*	Asterisk; Star	&#42;	&#x2a;	
+	Plus sign	&#43;	&#x2b;	
,	Comma	&#44;	&#x2c;	

Symbol	Description	Decimal Code	Hex Code	Special Code / Entity Name
-	Hyphen; Hyphen minus sign	&#45;	&#x2d;	
.	Period; Dot; Full stop	&#46;	&#x2e;	
/	Slash; Forward slash; Fraction bar	&#47;	&#x2f;	
0	Zero; 0	&#48;	&#x30;	
1	One; 1	&#49;	&#x31;	
2	Two; 2	&#50;	&#x32;	
3	Three; 3	&#51;	&#x33;	
4	Four; 4	&#52;	&#x34;	
5	Five; 5	&#53;	&#x35;	
6	Six; 6	&#54;	&#x36;	
7	Seven; 7	&#55;	&#x37;	
8	Eight; 8	&#56;	&#x38;	
9	Nine; 9	&#57;	&#x39;	
:	Colon	&#58;	&#x3a;	
;	Semicolon	&#59;	&#x3b;	
<	Less than symbol; Left angle bracket	&#60;	&#x3c;	&lt;
=	Equal sign; Equality symbol	&#61;	&#x3d;	
>	Greater than symbol; Right angle bracket	&#62;	&#x3e;	&gt;
?	Question mark	&#63;	&#x3f;	
@	At symbol	&#64;	&#x40;	
A	Capital A	&#65;	&#x41;	
B	Capital B	&#66;	&#x42;	
C	Capital C	&#67;	&#x43;	

Symbol	Description	Decimal Code	Hex Code	Special Code / Entity Name
D	Capital D	&#68;	&#x44;	
E	Capital E	&#69;	&#x45;	
F	Capital F	&#70;	&#x46;	
G	Capital G	&#71;	&#x47;	
H	Capital H	&#72;	&#x48;	
I	Capital I	&#73;	&#x49;	
J	Capital J	&#74;	&#x4a;	
K	Capital K	&#75;	&#x4b;	
L	Capital L	&#76;	&#x4c;	
M	Capital M	&#77;	&#x4d;	
N	Capital N	&#78;	&#x4e;	
O	Capital O	&#79;	&#x4f;	
P	Capital P	&#80;	&#x50;	
Q	Capital Q	&#81;	&#x51;	
R	Capital R	&#82;	&#x52;	
S	Capital S	&#83;	&#x53;	
T	Capital T	&#84;	&#x54;	
U	Capital U	&#85;	&#x55;	
V	Capital V	&#86;	&#x56;	
W	Capital W	&#87;	&#x57;	
X	Capital X	&#88;	&#x58;	
Y	Capital Y	&#89;	&#x59;	
Z	Capital Z	&#90;	&#x5a;	
[	Left square bracket	&#91;	&#x5b;	
\	Backslash	&#92;	&#x5c;	
]	Right square bracket	&#93;	&#x5d;	
^	Caret	&#94;	&#x5e;	

Symbol	Description	Decimal Code	Hex Code	Special Code / Entity Name
_	Underscore; Understrike; Underbar; Underline	_	_	
`	Grave accent	`	`	
a	Lower case a	a	a	
b	Lower case b	b	b	
c	Lower case c	c	c	
d	Lower case d	d	d	
e	Lower case e	e	e	
f	Lower case f	f	f	
g	Lower case g	g	g	
h	Lower case h	h	h	
i	Lower case i	i	i	
j	Lower case j	j	j	
k	Lower case k	k	k	
l	Lower case l	l	l	
m	Lower case m	m	m	
n	Lower case n	n	n	
o	Lower case o	o	o	
p	Lower case p	p	p	
q	Lower case q	q	q	
r	Lower case r	r	r	
s	Lower case s	s	s	
t	Lower case t	t	t	
u	Lower case u	u	u	
v	Lower case v	v	v	
w	Lower case w	w	w	
x	Lower case x	x	x	

Symbol	Description	Decimal Code	Hex Code	Special Code / Entity Name
y	Lower case y	&#121;	&#x79;	
z	Lower case z	&#122;	&#x7a;	
{	Left curly brace; Left curly bracket	&#123;	&#x7b;	
|	Vertical bar; Pipe; Sheffer stroke; Absolute value symbol; Norm symbol; Nand symbol; Or symbol; Solid vertical bar	&#124;	&#x7c;	
}	Right curly brace; Right curly bracket	&#125;	&#x7d;	
~	Tilde; Mathematical similar symbol; Mathematical equivalent symbol; Logical negation symbol	&#126;	&#x7e;	
[]	Delete control character	&#127;	&#x7f;	
	Non-breaking space			
¡	Inverted exclamation point; Inverted exclamation mark	&#161;	&#xa1;	&iexcl;
¢	Cent symbol	&#162;	&#xa2;	&cent;
£	Lira sign	&#163;	&#xa3;	&pound;

Symbol	Description	Decimal Code	Hex Code	Special Code / Entity Name
¤	General currency sign	&#164;	&#xa4;	&curren;
¥	Japanese Yen currency sign; Yen symbol	&#165;	&#xa5;	&yen;
¦	Broken vertical bar; Pipe; Sheffer stroke; Broken bar	&#166;	&#xa6;	&brvbar;
§	Section sign; Double S; Sectional symbol	&#167;	&#xa7;	§ or Alt-21 on the number pad
¨	Umlaut; Dieresis	&#168;	&#xa8;	¨ or ¨
©	Copyright symbol; Copr symbol	&#169;	&#xa9;	&copy;
ª	Feminine ordinal indicator	&#170;	&#xaa;	&ordf;
«	Left angle quotation marks	&#171;	&#xab;	&laquo;
¬	Logical negation symbol; Logical complement; Not symbol	&#172;	&#xac;	&not;
®	Registered trademark symbol	&#174;	&#xae;	&reg;
¯	Macron accent; Macron symbol; Macron	&#175;	&#xaf;	&macr;
°	Degree sign; Degree symbol	&#176;	&#xb0;	&deg;
±	Plus or minus	&#177;	&#xb1;	&plusmn;
²	Superscript 2; Exponent 2	&#178;	&#xb2;	&sup2;

Symbol	Description	Decimal Code	Hex Code	Special Code / Entity Name
³	Superscript 3; Exponent 3	&#179;	&#xb3;	&sup3;
´	Acute accent; Sharp accent; High accent	&#180;	&#xb4;	&acute;
µ	Lower case Greek letter mu; Science symbol for micro; µ	&#181;	&#xb5;	&micro;
¶	Paragraph symbol; pilcrow; Blind P; Paragraph mark; Paraph; Alinea	&#182;	&#xb6;	¶ or Alt-20 on the number pad
·	Middle dot; Interpunct; Interpoint; Dot operator; Dot product operator; Fullwidth; Inner dot; Ponch naut	&#183;	&#xb7;	&middot;
¸	Cedilla; Cedilha; cédille; Hook tail	&#184;	&#xb8;	&cedil;
¹	Superscript 1; Exponent 1	&#185;	&#xb9;	&sup1;
º	Masculine ordinal indicator	&#186;	&#xba;	&ordm;
»	Right angle quotation marks	&#187;	&#xbb;	&raquo;
¼	Fraction 1/4; Fraction one fourth	&#188;	&#xbc;	&frac14;
½	Fraction 1/2; Fraction one half	&#189;	&#xbd;	&frac12;

Symbol	Description	Decimal Code	Hex Code	Special Code / Entity Name
¾	Fraction 3/4; Fraction three quarters	&#190;	&#xbe;	&frac34;
¿	Inverted question mark	&#191;	&#xbf;	&iquest;
À	Capital A, grave accent	&#192;	&#xc0;	&Agrave;
Á	Capital A acute accent	&#193;	&#xc1;	&Aacute;
Â	Capital A circumflex accent	&#194;	&#xc2;	&Acirc;
Ã	Capital A tilde	&#195;	&#xc3;	&Atilde;
Ä	Capital A umlaut, Capital A dieresis mark	&#196;	&#xc4;	&Auml;
Å	Capital A ring	&#197;	&#xc5;	&Aring;
Æ	Capital AE ligature; Dipthong; Aesc; Ash	&#198;	&#xc6;	&Aelig;
Ç	Capital C cedilla	&#199;	&#xc7;	&Ccedil;
È	Capital E grave accent	&#200;	&#xc8;	&Egrave;
É	Capital E acute accent	&#201;	&#xc9;	&Eacute;
Ê	Capital E circumflex accent	&#202;	&#xca;	&Ecirc;
Ë	Capital E umlaut; Capital E dieresis mark	&#203;	&#xcb;	&Euml;
Ì	Capital I grave accent	&#204;	&#xcc;	&Igrave;

Symbol	Description	Decimal Code	Hex Code	Special Code / Entity Name
Í	Capital I acute accent	&#205;	&#xcd;	&Iacute;
Î	Capital I circumflex accent	&#206;	&#xce;	&Icirc;
Ï	Capital I umlaut; Capital I dieresis mark	&#207;	&#xcf;	&Iuml;
Ð	Capital Eth, Icelandic; Capital Edh; D-stroke	&#208;	&#xd0;	&ETH;
Ñ	Capital N tilde; Capital enye	&#209;	&#xd1;	&Ntilde;
Ò	Capital O grave accent	&#210;	&#xd2;	&Ograve;
Ó	Capital O acute accent	&#211;	&#xd3;	&Oacute;
Ô	Capital O circumflex accent	&#212;	&#xd4;	&Ocirc;
Õ	Capital O tilde	&#213;	&#xd5;	&Otilde;
Ö	Capital O umlaut; Capital O dieresis mark	&#214;	&#xd6;	&Ouml;
×	Multiplication symbol; Times sign; St. Anderew's Cross; Dimension sign; Into sign	&#215;	&#xd7;	&times;
Ø	Capital O slash; Empty set symbol; Nullset symbol; Null set	&#216;	&#xd8;	Ø, \varnothing in TeX, or \empty in TeX

Symbol	Description	Decimal Code	Hex Code	Special Code / Entity Name
Ù	Capital U grave accent	Ù	Ù	Ù
Ú	Capital S-comma	Ú	Ú	
Û	Lowercase s-comma	Û	Û	
Ü	Capital U umlaut; Capital U dieresis mark	Ü	Ü	Ü
Ý	Capital Y acute accent	Ý	Ý	Ý
Þ	Capital Thorn, Icelandic; Middle English Th	Þ	Þ	Þ
ß	Small sz ligature, German; Eszett; Scharfes S; Sharp S	ß	ß	ß
à	Lower case a grave accent	à	à	à
á	Lower case a acute accent	á	á	á
â	Lower case a circumflex accent	â	â	â
ã	Lower case a tilde	ã	ã	ã
ä	Lower case umlaut; Lower case a dieresis mark	ä	ä	ä
å	Lower case a ring	å	å	å
æ	Lower case ae ligature; Dipthong	æ	æ	æ

Symbol	Description	Decimal Code	Hex Code	Special Code / Entity Name
ç	Lower case c cedilla	&#231;	&#xe7;	&ccedil;
è	Lower case e grave accent	&#232;	&#xe8;	&egrave;
é	Lower case e acute accent	&#233;	&#xe9;	&eacute;
ê	Lower case e circumflex accent	&#234;	&#xea;	&ecirc;
ë	Lower case e umlaut; Lower case e dieresis mark	&#235;	&#xeb;	&euml;
ì	Lower case i grave accent	&#236;	&#xec;	&igrave;
í	Lower case i acute accent	&#237;	&#xed;	&iacute;
î	Lower case i circumflex accent	&#238;	&#xee;	&icirc;
ï	Lower case i umlaut; Lower case i dieresis	&#239;	&#xef;	&iuml;
ð	Lower case eth, Icelandic; Lower case edh	&#240;	&#xf0;	&eth;
ñ	Lower case n tilde; Lower case enye	&#241;	&#xf1;	&ntilde;
ò	Lower case o grave accent	&#242;	&#xf2;	&ograve;
ó	Lower case o acute accent	&#243;	&#xf3;	&oacute;

Symbol	Description	Decimal Code	Hex Code	Special Code / Entity Name
ô	Lower case o circumflex accent	&#244;	&#xf4;	&ocirc;
õ	Lower case o tilde	&#245;	&#xf5;	&otilde;
ö	Lower case o umlaut; Lower case o dieresis	&#246;	&#xf6;	&ouml;
÷	Division symbol; Obelus; Division sign	&#247;	&#xf7;	&divide;
ø	Lower case o slash; Empty set symbol; Nullset symbol; Null set	&#248;	&#xf8;	&oslash;
ù	Lower case u grave accent	&#249;	&#xf9;	&ugrave;
ú	Lower case u acute accent	&#250;	&#xfa;	&uacute;
û	Lower case u circumflex accent	&#251;	&#xfb;	&ucirc;
ü	Lower case u umlaut; Lower case u dieresis	&#252;	&#xfc;	&uuml;
ý	Lower case y acute accent	&#253;	&#xfd;	&yacute;
þ	Lower case thorn, Icelandic; Middle English th	&#254;	&#xfe;	&thorn;
ÿ	Lower case y umlaut; Lower case y dieresis mark	&#255;	&#xff;	&yuml;

Zodiac Sign Symbols

Symbol	Description	Decimal Code	Hex Code	Special Code / Entity Name
♈	Aries ♈	♈	♈	
♉	Taurus ♉	♉	♉	
♊	Gemini ♊	♊	♊	
♋	Cancer ♋	♋	♋	
♌	Leo ♌	♌	♌	
♍	Virgo, minim ♍	♍	♍	
♎	Libra ♎	♎	♎	
♏	Scorpius, scorpio, minim ♏	♏	♏	
♐	Sagittarius ♐	♐	♐	
♑	Capricorn ♑	♑	♑	
♒	Aquarius ♒	♒	♒	
♓	Pisces ♓	♓	♓	
⛎	Ophiuchus ⛎	⛎	⛎	

Monkeys

Symbol	Description	Decimal Code	Hex Code	Special Code / Entity Name
🙈	Monkey see no evil 🙈	🙈	🙈	
🙉	Monkey hear no evil 🙉	🙉	🙉	
🙊	Monkey speak no evil 🙊	🙊	🙊	

Now that you know what HTML special characters are, let me know show you how to add HTML special characters to your web page in the example below.

```
<ul>
  <li>Monkey see no evil &#128584;</li>
  <li>Monkey hear no evil &#128585;</li>
  <li>Monkey speak no evil &#128586;</li>
</ul>
```

Example 201

Example as seen in FireFox 80.0.1 (64-bit) browser.

- Monkey see no evil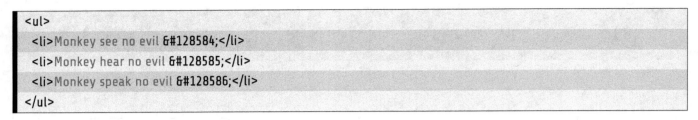
- Monkey hear no evil
- Monkey speak no evil

Reference List

- https://html.spec.whatwg.org/multipage/dom.html#content-models

- https://developer.mozilla.org/en-US/docs/Web/Guide/HTML/Content_categories

- https://dev.w3.org/html5/html-author/#categories

- http://www.addressmunger.com/special_ascii_characters/

- https://altcodeunicode.com/

www.ingramcontent.com/pod-product-compliance
Lightning Source LLC
LaVergne TN
LVHW081657050326
832903LV00026B/1801